Study Guide

for use with

Financial Markets and Institutions
A Modern Perspective

Second Edition

Anthony Saunders
New York University
Stern School of Business

Marcia Cornett
University of Southern Illinois

Prepared by
William Lepley
University of Wisconsin-Green Bay

 Irwin

Boston   Burr Ridge, IL   Dubuque, IA   Madison, WI   New York   San Francisco   St. Louis
Bangkok   Bogotá   Caracas   Kuala Lumpur   Lisbon   London   Madrid   Mexico City
Milan   Montreal   New Delhi   Santiago   Seoul   Singapore   Sydney   Taipei   Toronto

Study Guide for use with
Financial Markets and Institutions: A Modern Perspective
Anthony Saunders and Marcia Cornett

Published by McGraw-Hill/Irwin, an imprint of The McGraw-Hill Companies, Inc., 1221 Avenue of the Americas, New York, NY 10020. Copyright © 2004, 2001 by The McGraw-Hill Companies, Inc. All rights reserved.

1 2 3 4 5 6 7 8 9 0 BKM/BKM 0 9 8 7 6 5 4 3

ISBN 0-07-282457-3

www.mhhe.com

The McGraw-Hill Companies

CHAPTER 0

In case you haven't figured it out yet, this *Study Guide* is designed to help the users of *Financial Markets and Institutions, A Modern Perspective*, second edition, by Anthony Saunders and Marcia Millon Cornett. And this is... *Chapter 0*? Yes, this chapter is nothing. It's the *Rodney Dangerfield* of *Study Guide* chapters. It gets absolutely no respect. Why? Well, this is sort of like a "Preface." And, seriously now, when's the last time you actually read a book's *preface*? (Has anybody *ever* read one?)

What exactly does the *Study Guide* aim to accomplish? The same three things that the *first edition* set out to do:
1) Provide some practice with *word stuff*: terminology and descriptions.
2) Provide some practice with *number stuff*: problems.
3) To have a little fun, while accomplishing (1) and (2).

The first two things are the typical meat and potatoes of any study guide. But the third thing may be little *untypical*. Studying is often *hard* work. But just remember: the inhabitants of financial markets and institutions are human beings. They certainly try to "lighten things up" while doing their jobs. Why shouldn't we do the same?

To serve the goals above, I've tried to provide plenty of practice with the textbook material. There are questions on terminology and concepts, as well as lots of number-crunching problems (with solutions). But I've also tried, whenever possible, to present things in an informal, conversational way. I like to examine things from both a "big picture" vantage point, as well as down at "ground level." So, you *might* see the logic behind the organization for each chapter, presented below. (If you don't see it, something tells me this book is now on its way back to the store!)

I. Surveying the Territory: An Aerial View   **(Big picture stuff)**
II. Digging in the Dirt: A Subterranean View   **(Ground level stuff)**
     Got a question?   **(Terminology & essay questions)**
     Got a problem?   **(Fire up your calculator)**
     Web cruising ideas   **(Fire up your web browser)**
III. Washing Up... And the "ABC" Awards   **(Off the wall stuff)**
     A. The EASIEST THING in the chapter
     B. The HARDEST THING in the chapter
     C. The FUNNIEST THING in the chapter... or not
IV. Checking the Answers... For Section II   **(Students go here too quickly!)**

Before the fun begins...let me thank Sarah Ebel, Developmental Editor, for her support and encouragement. (And let me thank my wife and kids... for no particular reason... after all, they don't need a special reason.)

William Lepley

TABLE OF CONTENTS

CHAPTER 1
INTRODUCTION

I.   SURVEYING THE TERRITORY: AN AERIAL VIEW

Let's start by looking over the major topic headings for Chapter 1. In other words, let's see where Professors Saunders and Cornett are taking us.

Why Study Financial Markets and Institutions?: Chapter Overview

Overview of Financial Markets

Overview of Financial Institutions

Globalization of Financial Markets and Institutions

Now, that was simple enough. Markets…Institutions…okay, we've just read the title of the book again…after all, this is *Chapter 1*, right?   As with hundreds of other "Chapter 1s" in the world of textbooks, the most popular word is probably *overview*. There can't be much going on here, right? The authors are just telling us what will happen *later*, right?

Well, *yes*… they do tell us what's coming later on.

But *no*…there's some real *stuff* here. You know what I'm talking about—the kind of stuff that can show up on an exam. So, don't dismiss it so quickly.

II.   DIGGING IN THE DIRT: A SUBTERRANEAN VIEW

To learn this stuff, you've got to do some digging. There are four kinds of things to cover here: (1) **key terms**, (2) **questions**—using words, rather than numbers, (3) **problems**—crunching some numbers, and (4) relevant **web site** information.

Let's go play in the dirt.

Key terms

> **financial markets**
> **primary market**
> **initial public offering**
> **derivative security**
> **private placement**
> **secondary market**
> **money market**
> **over-the-counter market**

capital market
spot foreign exchange transaction
forward foreign exchange transaction
financial institutions
direct transfer
liquidity
price risk
indirect transfer
monitoring costs
delegated monitor
asset transformers
diversify
economies of scale
etrade
maturity intermediation
denomination intermediation
transmission of monetary policy
credit allocation
intergenerational wealth transfers
time intermediation
payment services
Eurodollar bond

Now, if you want to get picky about it, we *could* come up with even *more* terms. But if you can understand this set, you'll be in decent shape.

Got a question?

For the initial ones, find the *term*—from the list above—which works best in the blank. Then you can try writing some *essays*. And what about some *answers*? Yes, you'll find them in a later section. But try the questions first. (By the way, there are just a handful of descriptions here—not one for each term in the list—so don't run back to the bookstore, insisting that you've been cheated out of a page!)

1. This is the market for longer-term funds. The key issue is the *time* for which the funds are provided. We "draw the line" at one year. So, if a security will pay back for a term greater than a year, it's in this market.
   This is the _____.

2. This is the market for "used" securities—i.e., like the used car market. So, the securities in this market are probably not being offered for sale by their original issuers.
   This is the _____.

3. This is the first offer of a company's securities to the public. These are brand-spanking-new securities.
   This is a _____.

4. Let's say a whole bunch of folks deposit, on average, $100 per week in the bank. Then, the bank periodically "bundles up" the money and lends it out in $10 thousand or even $100 thousand increments. (Clue: think about "size" here.)
   The bank is engaged in: _____.

5. When a bank lends out funds (as in the preceding question), it is performing a "surveillance" function on behalf of the depositors. After all, sometimes borrowers need to be "checked on," don't they?
   When the bank performs this function, it is acting as a _____.

6. With this market, *time* is the key characteristic of interest. Suppose a security is scheduled to be paid off in the short-term—let's say less than one year.
   The security is trading in the: _____.

7. Suppose you are a Federal Reserve economist—worrying about how money supply changes will influence the financial world, and ultimately, affect things like paychecks, inventories, and inflation.
   You are worried about the: _____.

8. Our friend Laura handles the chickens and eggs on her farm. When she collects the eggs, she is careful *not* to "put all her eggs in one basket." And, when she invests the money from selling the eggs, she tries to follow the same principle.
   Laura has chosen to: _____.

9. Think of a general term for businesses like commercial banks, credit unions, or insurance companies… but *not* including firms like Microsoft, Walmart, or Home Depot.
   We are talking about examples of: _____.

10. Jack's National Bank has a loan portfolio of $200 *million*. Jill's National Bank has a loan portfolio of $2 *billion*. Jill's average operating cost (say, per dollar of assets) is lower than Jack's average cost of operating.
    This demonstrates the phenomenon of: _____.

11. Bernie doesn't deal with banks. But he sometimes lends a few bucks to his friend Barney, who pays Bernie back on payday. This kind of transaction is a:
    _____.

12. Derrick Industries Inc. is selling bonds. No underwriters are involved; instead, Derrick is selling the bonds directly to investors. This is an example of a:
    _____.

13. Consider this statement: "Secondary market transactions have no consequences for the original *issuers* of securities, because the issuers receive no funding from such transactions." Do you agree or disagree? Explain.

14. Distinguish a *forward* foreign exchange transaction from a *spot* foreign exchange transaction.

15. Contrast a *commercial bank* with a *thrift institution*. Also, how important have they been in the U.S.—in terms of their size *relative to* the overall financial institution sector?

16. Which seems most important in the U.S.: *direct transfers* or *indirect transfers*? Why?

17. In August 2001, one economist, commenting on events in the NASDAQ Stock Market, said: "...with the benefit of hindsight, the late 90s never happened." What was this economist driving at?

Got a problem?

You will probably be happy to know that we *don't* have a problem here! After all, this is still Chapter 1. If you *are* disappointed, relax. There's more to come... and the textbook is a mighty big one.

Web cruising ideas

Even though we're in the introductory chapter, it's not a bad idea to get your fingers limbered up—and start clicking around to see what's available on the World Wide Web.

1. The New York Stock Exchange has an extensive web site. The home page is:

   http://www.nyse.com/

2. One of the specific areas at the NYSE site is related to market information. Try this page:

   http://www.nyse.com/marketinfo/marketinfo.html

Here, you can access the latest market pricing information, but there are also hot buttons for other data, as well as research. (You might be able to uncover some research papers that would help you with *your* research papers.)

3. The text's Table 1-9 shows data from the Federal Reserve's "Flow of Funds" accounts. As with so many things these days, you can retrieve up-to-date

information on the web. The home page for he Board of Governors of the Federal Reserve System is:

http://www.federalreserve.gov/

Look for "Economic Research and Data" link, if you want the latest economic data—or, for that matter, lots of old data as well.

III. WASHING UP... AND THE "ABC" AWARDS

Hey, my hands are downright filthy... so let's wash up and shoot the... well you know....

A. The EASIEST THING in the chapter

Table 1-4, listing different types of financial institutions. I'm guessing most readers already understand at least three-quarters of these. If not, then you probably just arrived from another planet. Still, it's useful to look them over—and, see if you can determine where the various institutions around you "fit in" on the list.

B. The HARDEST THING in the chapter

I'd say its all those darn risks, as listed in **Table 1-7**. How *anybody* could *really* understand—and distinguish among—all those risks at this point is beyond me. But remember: this is Chapter 1. Study **Table 1-7**, and know this: you *will* visit these risks again!

C. The FUNNIEST THING in the chapter... or not

Ever notice the human capacity for coming up with a high-minded term to describe wha+t might be a rather unpleasant activity? Here are two, related ones: ***monitoring costs*** and ***delegated monitor***. Now the "monitoring" implied here is an absolute necessity in the financial world. What goes on? Well, when I use *other people's money*, those *other people* are going to be snooping around, trying to determine exactly what I'm up to. They're checking up on me. They might have to get downright *nosey*, in fact. And that's the point: ***monitoring*** does sound a whole lot better than ***snooping***—and maybe a bit more professional, too. (How would *you* like to be known as Senior Vice President for Snooping Activities, at Last National Bank?)

IV.   CHECKING THE ANSWERS... FOR SECTION II

Terms:

1. capital market
2. secondary market
3. initial public offering (and, you can also say this is a *primary market* transaction)
4. denomination intermediation
5. delegated monitor
6. money market
7. transmission of monetary policy
8. diversify
9. financial institutions
10. economies of scale
11. direct transfer
12. private placement

Essays:

13. It is true that secondary market transactions do not generate funds for the issuers. Secondary market transactions occur *after* the primary market transactions. However, secondary market transactions *are important* to security issuers. The mere *existence* of secondary market activity can make it easier for issuers to sell their securities in the primary market. Investors value liquidity, and if they see an active secondary market, they will be more willing to purchase securities in the primary market. In addition, secondary market activity provides useful provides *pricing* information. The prices allow the issuers to gauge how investors are evaluating or "grading" their decisions on allocating the funds. The pricing information is also useful if the issuer is considering the sale of more securities.

14. Both transactions obviously involve the trade of one currency (say U.S. dollars) for another currency (say Japanese yen). The difference has to do with *when* the currencies will change hands. With a *spot* transaction, the dollars and yen change hands at the time of the agreement—you might say it changes hands "on the spot." In contrast, with a *forward* transaction, the dollars and yen will change hands some time *after* the deal has been struck. The deal has been made *in advance* of the actual money flow. A delivery date will be specified in the forward transaction, indicating when the currencies will change hands.

15. Both thrifts and commercial banks are *depository institutions*—meaning that issuance of *deposit* liabilities is a primary way of raising funds. But thrift institutions have been more specialized in terms of where they invest their funds. Savings institutions, for example, direct their funding towards home mortgage lending. Credit unions, another type of thrift, have a consumer loan focus. Commercial banks have typically been involved in a broader array of lending—business loans, consumer loans, and mortgage loans. Both thrifts and commercial banks have been very significant in terms of asset size, although in recent years, their relative shares have fallen. In 1948, for example, combined assets of thrifts and commercial banks amounted to about 68

percent of overall financial institution assets. By 2001, their share had fallen to about 46 percent (see Table 1-5 in the text). Commercial banks, by themselves, have shown a dramatic, long-term fall in relative asset size—from a 60-plus percent share in the early 1900s to 35.8 percent in 2001. Both of these institution classes remain important, but other institutional types have been growing.

16. A *direct transfer* occurs when a supplier of funds deals *directly* with someone who wants to use the funds (for example, a loan from you to your brother-in-law). With *indirect transfers*, a financial institution is involved in the process—linking up suppliers and users of funds, who never even have to see each other. John deposits his paycheck in Rock Solid Savings Bank. Then, Mary goes to Rock Solid and borrows the funds (along with funds from other suppliers), to finance a home purchase. In the industrialized world, *indirect transfers* seem clearly to be the dominant type. The reasons relate to the costs and risks of direct transfers. Liquidity and default risks can loom large, but financial institutions can become very good at dealing with these risks. The *transactions costs* involved in bringing supplier and demander together—and, in particular, the *monitoring costs*—provide an important rationale for financial institution existence. Financial institutions can economize on these costs.

17. The economist's quotation comes from the beginning of Chapter 1. In particular, *The Wall Street Journal* (August 16, 2001) was reporting on the recent four quarters of losses for about 4200 NASDAQ firms. The reported losses just about equaled the gains that had been turned in for the period starting in September 1995.

CHAPTER 2
DETERMINANTS OF INTEREST RATES

I.   SURVEYING THE TERRITORY: AN AERIAL VIEW

In this chapter, we see *interest rates* from over, under, sideways, and more. But to start, just remember a couple of basic things. First, *interest*—whether it's in dollars, yen, pounds, or even some *real* asset—is just a sort of payment or "bribe" designed to get one person to willingly *do without* something for a period of time. I give someone $100, thereby foregoing the opportunity to spend it now. In return, I hope to get back my $100, *plus interest,* next year.

The person who "does without" is the *lender*. It could be the person who buys a bond from General Motors. It could also be an eight year-old boy, who puts five bucks in a savings account at the local bank. (Of course, the boy probably doesn't view himself as a lender—even though he is, most definitely, lending money to the bank. And the GM bond-holder might refer herself as an *investor*.)

The person who gets the "something"—at least for a while—is the *borrower*. And what's the price for all this? Well, that's where the interest payment comes in—and the *interest rate* merely expresses the interest payment as a percentage of the amount loaned.

Here are the chapter's main topics. (And yes…in case you were wondering… this list, when coupled with 79 cents, will buy you a *really bad* cup of coffee.)

Interest Rate Fundamentals: Chapter Overview

Time Value of Money and Interest Rates

Loanable Funds Theory

Movement of Interest Rates Over Time

Determinants of Interest Rates for Individual Securities

Term Structure of Interest Rates

Forecasting Interest Rates

II.   DIGGING IN THE DIRT: A SUBTERRANEAN VIEW

Key terms

> nominal interest rate
> time value of money
> compound interest
> simple interest
> present value
> lump sum payment
> annuity
> future value
> equivalent annual return
> discount yield
> single payment yield
> loanable funds theory
> supply of funds
> demand for funds
> on-the-run
> off-the-run
> equilibrium interest rate
> inflation
> real interest rate
> Fisher effect
> default risk
> liquidity risk
> special provisions, or covenants
> taxability
> convertibility
> callability
> term structure of interest rates
> yield curve
> unbiased expectations theory
> liquidity premium theory
> market segmentation theory
> preferred habitat theory
> forward rate

Got a question?

1. Linda is thinking about buying a bond. But a primary concern is the bond's limited marketability. If she buys it, she may not be able to turn it back into cash in a hurry.
    This risk is called: _____.

2. Larry bought a house, financing it with a 30-year mortgage loan. The loan allows Larry to "pre-pay"—paying off the full balance—without penalty. The loan has an interest rate of 10%. If Larry had instead taken a loan that *could not* be paid off early, the lender would have charged an interest rate of 9.5%. The interest rate on Larry's loan has a premium based on: _____.

3. Sphinx Corp. Bond is a straight bond, and was issued today with an interest rate of 10%. King Corp. Bond was also issued a straight bond today, at an interest rate of 10.5%. The Sphinx Bond and the King Bond have the same *default risk*. Also, the two bonds are the same in terms of their special provisions and covenants. The difference in interest rates is probably attributable to the: _____.

4. A dollar received *today* is worth more to me than a dollar received *a year from now*
This is the essence of the: _____.

5. As businesses foresee increasingly profitable investment opportunities, they desire more financing. They may offer securities in the marketplace to raise money. This is an important factor behind the: _____.

6. Suppose the quantity of funds demanded is equal to the quantity of funds supplied. The resulting interest rate would be the: _____.

7. Today, we observe and record the yields on bonds of *different* maturity—but sharing the same credit risk, taxability, and special provisions or covenants. The graph of the yields against corresponding maturities is the: _____.

8. Julie has $1,000 to put in the bank. Given the bank's interest rate, she will have $1,050 in exactly one year. In "time value of money" jargon, the $1,050 amount is a: _____.

9. To lease his new car, Mark will be paying $475 per month for 48 months. This flow of payments is an example of an: _____.

10. A municipal bond's yield will typically be *lower* than the yield on a corporate bond even if the default risk and callability are identical. The yield difference is most likely due to: _____.

11. In the face of news of increased inflation, and an expectation of further price increases in coming years, we observe an increase in long-term bond yields. An interest rate impact such as this has been termed the: _____.

12. _____ Treasury securities are being offered to the market for the first time. In contrast, _____ Treasury securities are previously issued securities.

13. Suppose the business outlook turns gloomy. We aren't exactly sure what started it, but consumers are not eager to buy new products. Retailers see their inventories build up, so they postpone orders for new items. Producers cut back on orders for raw materials. In the context of the "loanable funds theory," what happens to the *demand for funds*? From this, explain what would happen to the level of interest rates.

14. Sometimes, in the face of a troubling general economic picture, bond market participants exhibit something called a "flight to quality." Can you guess who's flying *where*? And *why* they might want to fly there? (Think about: negative economic news, and its impact on investor behavior.)

15. As we look at some actual interest rates from *different* parts of the financial markets—as in the text's **Figure 2-12**—what sort of relationship seems apparent?

16. Use the loanable funds framework to explain what happens if market participants perceive *higher* default risk for bonds.

Got a problem?

Yes, we do—more than one, in fact.

1. Wanda has $2,500 to put in the bank. Two local banks, East Bank and West Bank, are both paying a stated interest rate of 4% annually. But East Bank compounds **quarterly**, and West Bank compounds **daily**. How much will Wanda have in her account:
   a) After 1 year, if interest is compounded quarterly—as at East Bank?
   b) After 5 years, if interest is compounded quarterly—as at East Bank?
   c) After 1 year, if interest is compounded daily—as at West Bank?
   d) After 5 years, if interest is compounded daily—as at West Bank?

2. Referring to the preceding problem:
   a) What is the equivalent annual rate (or "effective annual rate," or just EAR) at East Bank?
   b) What is the EAR at West Bank?

3. Wanda (see preceding problems) discovers yet another bank. This one also pays 4% annually, but it compounds continuously. If Wanda deposits her $2,500 in this bank,
   a) How much will she have in her account after 1 year?
   b) How much will she have in her account after 5 years?
   c) What is the equivalent annual rate (EAR) on this account?

4. Max wants to make a bank deposit of sufficient size so that he will have $15,000 in exactly 6 years. If his bank will pay him 5%, compounded monthly, what amount does Max have to deposit today?

5. Justin Leasing is leasing out some equipment for $12,000 per month, payable for the next 4 years. The payments are made at the end of each month. If the simple annual interest rate on the investment is 8%, what is the present value of this payment stream?
(Clue: See text Example 2-4.)

6. Referring back to the preceding question, suppose Justin Leasing invests each of the monthly payments at the same simple annual interest rate (8%). Justin invests each payment as soon as it is received. What is the future value of this stream of payments—in exactly 4 years?
(Clue: see text Example 2-5.)

7. A $10,000 Treasury bill is currently selling for $9,850 and it has 45 days to maturity.
   a) Compute its **discount yield.**
   b) Compute its **bond equivalent yield.**
   c) Compute its **equivalent annual return.**
   (Clue: see text **Example 2-7.**)

8. Assume the Unbiased Expectations Hypothesis is true. Also, suppose that we pick up a Wall Street Journal and observe the following Treasury yields:
   > 11.00% on a 1-year bond
   > 12.00% on a 2-year bond
   > 11.50% on a 3-year bond

   a) Compute the implied one-year forward rate, for the period starting one year from now.
   b) Compute the implied one-year forward rate, for the period starting two years from now.
   c) How would you *interpret* the forward rates just computed? In other words, what's a way of describing the source of those rates, given the expectations hypothesis?
   (Clue: see text **Example 2-13.**)

9. Assume the Unbiased Expectations Hypothesis is true. We observe a 1-year Treasury yield of 3%. Suppose the market is expecting the 1-year interest rate to be 4% in one year, and 5% in two years. Find the following yields:
   a) On a 2-year security, right *now*.
   b) On a 3-year security, right *now*.

10. We observe a 6% interest rate on a 1-year Treasury security. We observe a 7.5% rate on a 2-year Treasury. Suppose we are confident that the market is expecting that the 1-year Treasury rate, a year from now, will be 8%. If the Liquidity Preference Theory is true, what is the liquidity premium for the second year of our horizon?

Web cruising ideas

1. There is so much financial data out there, where do we begin? One good, reputable place to start is the Federal Reserve Bank of St. Louis web site. In particular, go to their FRED page, and click away!

   http://research.stlouisfed.org/fred/index.html

2. Web sites can be good, bad…and sometimes very misleading. It's become really inexpensive to put information *out there*. But unfortunately, the information often *stays* out there, even when it's stale. Be skeptical of sites that try to provide links to "everything you'll ever want to know" about something. Getting information *close to the source* is important.

   Now, having issued that warning…here are a couple of reasonable places to find links to lots of financial data:

   http://finance.yahoo.com/

   http://moneycentral.msn.com/home.asp

III.   WASHING UP... AND THE "ABC" AWARDS

A. The EASIEST THING in the chapter

Well, it's **not easy** to find "easiness" in this chapter. But we'll say it's the historical movement of interest rates over time—as captured nicely by **Figure 2-12**. Really, how can you find fault with the plain, hard facts?

B. The HARDEST THING in the chapter

There are several good competitors in this race. But, over the years, many students have "met their Waterloo" at the **Battle to Understand the Loanable Funds Theory**. It really shouldn't be that way. But basic supply and demand analysis has put many good souls to the test. (Consolation prize: The **term structure** material comes in a very close second place.)

C. The FUNNIEST THING in the chapter...or not

Check yourself on the following stream of logic:

- We, as investors, like to earn *more* interest, right? **Check.**
- Now, suppose A-Jacks Company is in financial distress—meaning A-Jacks is having a hard time making its payments, pure and simple. **Check.**
- News like this travels fast. You find out. I find out. All God's children find out. The yield on the company's bonds *rises*, because of the perceived *higher* likelihood of default. **Check.**
- Okay, now suppose I'm one of the A-Jacks bond owners. **Check.**

   Now get ready...here's the punch line...

- I'm just as happy as a clam because the yield on my bonds went up. **Check... Uh ... NO CHECK!**

Now, most of you wise folks were *not* suckered into the trap there. But for those who fell for it, remember: when the default risk went up, the **price** of my bond fell. The **price** (or **value**) of something I owned went down. So, I'm *not* happy at all. In fact, that falling price provided the driving force for the bond's **rising yield**.

Okay, it's not exactly hilarious. But such streams of "illogic" have kept finance professors chuckling for years, as they grade exams. (They really ought to get out more.)

IV.   CHECKING THE ANSWERS... FOR SECTION II

Terms:
1. liquidity risk
2. callability (and there could be additional things creating a premium too)
3. the yield curve, or the term structure of interest rates (i.e., differing maturity)
4. time value of money
5. demand for funds
6. equilibrium interest rate
7. yield curve (or a graph of the "term structure")
8. future value
9. annuity
10. taxability (a specific case of "special provisions")
11. Fisher effect
12. on-the-run; off-the-run

Essays:
13. The factors described would suggest a *lower demand* for loanable funds. In graphic terms, the demand for funds curve would shift to the *left*. Producers do not need as much financing, because they are not producing as much. The reduced demand for funds would suggest a *lower* equilibrium interest rate.

14. A "flight to quality" (or "flight to safety") occurs when security holders sell higher risk securities and move into lower risk securities. For example, a holder of junk bonds sells them, and invests in higher quality corporate bonds or U.S. Treasury securities. Or, perhaps stockholders liquidate some of their holdings and move into the lower risk portion of the bond market. Why would it occur? The "flight" is likely to be prompted by fears of an economic recession—something that puts issuers in greater danger of *not* meeting their obligations.

15. In Figure 2-12, we see four different U.S. interest rates plotted for the period 1972-02—the prime rate, the T-bill rate, the high-grade corporate rate, and mortgage rates. The most striking thing is that the various rates *tend* to *move together*. They show positive correlation, at least when viewed over the long run. (But the rates are certainly not perfectly correlated.)

16. If bonds have greater default risk, then the *suppliers* of funds would be less willing to buy bonds—i.e., the *supply of funds* is reduced. In graphic terms, this would amount to a leftward shift of the *supply curve*. The result would be a higher equilibrium interest rate. Keep in mind that we are *starting* with the premise of *higher default risk*. That is what prompts the *shift* in supply.

Problems:

1. These are all "future value of a lump sum" problems.

    a) $FV = \$2,500\left(1 + .04\middle/4\right)^4 = \$2,601.51$

    Or, with future value notation,

    $FV = \$2.500\left(FVIF_{4\%/4,4}\right) = \$2,500 \times 1.04060 = \$2,601.51$

    The FVIF notation (or PVIF, for present value problems) is starting to look a big old-fashioned. It goes back to the days when we would typically be looking up these factors in a table. But there are limitations to tables—especially if you want to deal efficiently with real-world problems. The modern calculator does have its advantages!

    b) Now, we compound over more periods:

    $FV = \$2,500\left(1 + .04\middle/4\right)^{4\times5} = \$3,050.48$

    and, using future value notation,

    $FV = \$2.500\left(FVIF_{4\%/4,20}\right) = \$2,500 \times 1.22019 = \$3,050.48$

    c) Now, we compound more frequently in each year:

    $FV = \$2,500\left(1 + .04\middle/365\right)^{365} = \$2,602.02$

    d) Now, we compound more frequently, and also, over more years:

    $FV = \$2,500\left(1 + .04\middle/365\right)^{365\times5} = \$3,053.47$

2. Equivalent annual rate (EAR):

    a) At East Bank: $EAR = \left[1 + .04\middle/4\right]^4 - 1 = \ 0.0406 = 4.06\%$

    b) At West Bank: $EAR = \left[1 + .04\middle/365\right]^{365} - 1 = \ 0.04081 = 4.081\%$

3. For continuous compounding, note that the number of compounding periods ("m" in the textbook's equations) goes to infinity. In that case, the future value equation looks a bit different—employing that "mystery e" key on your calculator! (Well, it's not much of a mystery for the mathematically inclined.)

a) $FV = \$2,500e^{.04} = \$2,602.03$

b) $FV = \$2,500e^{.04 \times 5} = \$3,053.51$

c) $EAR = e^{.04} - 1 = 0.4081 = 4.081\%$

By the way, note that we've carried the EAR to three decimal places—and, to that point, the EAR with continuous compounding is indistinguishable from the EAR with daily compounding (see problem 2, part b). But if you split hairs—adding another decimal place or two—you will find that the EAR for the continuous compounding case is *slightly* larger.

4. This constitutes a "present value of a lump sum" problem.

$$PV = \$15,000 \frac{1}{\left(1 + .05/12\right)^{12 \times 6}} = \$11,119.20$$

Or, in present value notation:

$$PV = \$15,000\left(PVIF_{5\%/12,72}\right) = \$11,119.20$$

5. Take the present value of the 48 lease payments. The *per-period* discount rate is 8%, divided by 12. Writing out things the long way:

$$PV = \frac{\$12,000}{\left(1 + .08/12\right)} + \frac{\$12,000}{\left(1 + .08/12\right)^2} + \ldots + \frac{\$12,000}{\left(1 + .08/12\right)^{48}}$$

Or, using the "present value interest factor of an annuity" abbreviation:

$$PV = \$12,000\left(PVIFA_{8\%/12,48}\right) = \$491,542.96$$

6. Here, we are converting the payments to *future values*.

$$FV = \$12,000\left(1 + .08/12\right)^{47} + \$12,000\left(1 + .08/12\right)^{46} + \ldots + \$12,000\left(1 + .08/12\right) + \$12,000$$

$$FV = \$12,000\left(FVIFA_{8\%/12,48}\right) = \$676,198.98$$

7. For the $10,000 bill, currently selling for $9,850:

a) Discount: $DY = \dfrac{\$10,000 - \$9,850}{\$10,000} \times \dfrac{360}{45} = .12 = 12\%$

b) Bond equivalent: $BE = \dfrac{\$10,000 - \$9,850}{\$9,850} \times \dfrac{365}{45} = .1235 = 12.35\%$

c) Equivalent annual: $EAR = \left(1 + \dfrac{.1235}{365/45}\right)^{365/45} - 1 = .1304 = 13.04\%$

8. The basic idea here is that the long-term, short-term, and *forward* rates are linked together—by means of a "geometric average" equation.

a) For the period starting in one year, use the equation below—where $_1R_1$ is the currently observed 1-year rate. The left subscript indicates "where we are now" on some arbitrary time line. The subscript to the right indicates the maturity for the interest rate in question. So, $_1R_2$ is the interest rate, observed at time 1, for a 2-year maturity. And $_2f_1$ is the implied 1-year forward rate for the second year on our horizon.

$$_1R_2 = \left[(1 + {}_1R_1) \times (1 + {}_2f_1)\right]^{1/2} - 1$$

Plugging in the numbers:

$$.12 = \left[(1 + .11) \times (1 + {}_2f_1)\right]^{1/2} - 1$$

Solving for $_2f_1$:

$$_2f_1 = \left[(1.12)^2 / (1.11)\right] - 1 = .1301 = 13.01\%$$

b) Now, we use an expanded version of the equation from part (a), as shown below. We're now interested in a forward rate for a period one year "farther out," labeled $_3f_1$.

$$_1R_3 = \left[(1 + {}_1R_1) \times (1 + {}_2f_1) \times (1 + {}_3f_1)\right]^{1/3} - 1$$

Since, we have already solved for $_2f_1$ in part (a), it can be substituted in, and we can solve for $_3f_1$.

$$.115 = \left[(1.11) \times (1.1301) \times (1 + _3f_1)\right]^{\frac{1}{3}} - 1$$

Solving, we get $_3f_1 = .1051$ or 10.51%

c) In the expectations hypothesis, these "forward rates" are the same thing as the market's expected future spot interest rates.

9. This kind of problem emphasizes how—according to the Unbiased Expectations Hypothesis—the longer-term bond yields come about. Market expectations are driving them. We use the same equations as in the preceding problem, but now, our objective is different.

a) $_1R_2 = \left[(1 + _1R_1) \times (1 + _2f_1)\right]^{\frac{1}{2}} - 1$

$_1R_2 = \left[(1 + .03) \times (1 + .04)\right]^{\frac{1}{2}} - 1 = .03499 \approx 3.5\%$

b) $_1R_3 = \left[(1 + _1R_1) \times (1 + _2f_1) \times (1 + _3f_1)\right]^{\frac{1}{3}} - 1$

$_1R_3 = \left[(1 + .03) \times (1 + .04) \times (1 + .05)\right]^{\frac{1}{3}} - 1 = .03997 \approx 4\%$

10. Now, the relationship we used for the Unbiased Expectations Hypothesis is modified. The longer-term interest rates are driven by: (1) the current short-term interest rate, (2) the expected short-term rate, and (2) a liquidity premium. So, we have:

$$_1\overline{R}_2 = \left[(1 + _1\overline{R}_1) \times (1 + E(_2r_1) + L_2)\right]^{\frac{1}{2}} - 1$$

$$.075 = \left[(1 + .06) \times (1 + .08 + L_2)\right]^{\frac{1}{2}} - 1$$

Solving for L_2, we get 0.0102, or just slightly more than 1%. The longer-term rate ($_1R_2$ here) is affected by more than just the market expectation of the future spot interest rate. Investors demand a premium, to compensate for the "illiquidity" of the longer-term security.

CHAPTER 3
INTEREST RATES AND SECURITY VALUATION

I. SURVEYING THE TERRITORY: AN AERIAL VIEW

If you thought Chapter 2 was getting a bit "meaty" … well, we're in a *butcher shop* now. While Chapter 2 looked at interest rate determination, now we're reminded of *why* we care about those interest rates in the first place.

Changes in interest rates bring about changes in *values* of financial assets. And the impact of interest rates depends on the particular features of the stock, the bond, or whatever. Bottom line: if you own or manage things like stocks or bonds, you care about interest rate movements. And, you'll find Chapter 3 a useful part of your equipment.

Here are the chapter's major topics. *It's all about value.*

Interest Rates as a Determinant of Financial Security Values: Chapter Overview

Various Interest Rate Measures

Bond Valuation

Impact of Interest Rate Changes on Security Values

Impact of Maturity on Security Values

Impact of Coupon Rates on Security Values

Duration

II. DIGGING IN THE DIRT: A SUBTERRANEAN VIEW

Key terms

> **required rate of return**
> **fair present value**
> **expected rate of return**
> **realized rate of return**
> **coupon rate**
> **market efficiency**
> **coupon bond**
> **zero-coupon bond**
> **premium bond**
> **discount bond**

par bond
yield to maturity
price sensitivity
duration
elasticity
modified duration
convexity

You might note that the list of terms isn't quite so long this time around. But don't be fooled. The list may be shorter, but it's heavy.

Got a question?

1. This particular bond is priced at its par value. But remember, such a bond can be priced like this today, and priced very differently tomorrow. This is a:
   _____.

2. Consider a coupon-paying bond. Now, add up a full year's worth of coupon payments, and divide by the par value of the bond.
   When you do this, the result is: _____.

3. Investors conclude that Redland Corp.'s stock should earn a rate of return of 14%. They have determined this from their guesses about the stock's future prospects—any dividends and future price change—and their assessment of how risky those prospects are.
   The 14% return would be called: _____.

4. Still dealing with the preceding question's Redland Corp., suppose the investors' best guess about future cash flows, coupled with the stock's current price, suggest a 13% rate of return. In other words, 13% is our guess about the stock's future return if we buy *now*.
   The 13% return would be called: _____.

5. Referring one more time to Redland Corp., note that the returns in the two preceding questions are different. This difference will prompt investors to make trades, which, in turn, will cause Redland's stock price to change. The speed with which investors react and cause the price to change is the essence of the concept of: _____.

6. If we plotted a bond's *value* against different *yields to maturity*, and then played "connect the dots," our resulting picture would be a "curve."
   This demonstrates the bond pricing characteristic known as:
   _____.

7. Suppose we start with the text's formula for bond valuation, or:

$$V_b = \frac{INT}{m} \sum_{t=1}^{Nm} \left(\frac{1}{1 + \frac{i_d}{m}} \right)^t + \frac{M}{\left[1 + \frac{i_d}{m} \right]^{Nm}}$$

Now, suppose we put the actual *price* of a bond in the equation—for V_b. For INT, we put in the annual, promised coupon payment. For M, we put in the bond's par value. The "m" (note the small case here) is the number of times per year interest is paid, while N is the number of years to maturity. If we solve the equation for i_d, we will have the bond's: _____ .

8. This is a measurement related to an asset's maturity. It is the weighted average time to maturity on the asset.
   This measurement is called: _____ .

9. Start with duration, and then divide it by one plus the interest rate. This measurement, when multiplied by a the simple *change* in a bond's interest rate (the yield to maturity), will give us the approximate *percentage* change in the bond's price.
   This measurement is called: _____ .

10. **Duration** has a very practical, economic meaning to us: it is a/an _____ , which tells us the percentage change in an asset or liability value, for some small change in the interest rate.

11. Suppose you computed the **fair present value** of a security, by discounting to present value all the future, expected cash flows. And, you discount them at the appropriate "required rate of return."
    a) What if the fair present value is *not* equal to the going price for the security: explain what would be expected to happen.
    b) Further, explain how **market efficiency** relates to your answer from part (a).

Got a problem?

For problems 1-3, consider a bond issued by Bernice Corp., having the following characteristics:

Coupon rate:	8%
Payment frequency:	Semiannual
Maturity:	9 years
Par value:	$1,000
Required rate of return:	10%

1. Compute the bond's **fair present value**.

2. Still consider the bond from problem 1 above. Consider how the **fair present value** changes when the **required rate of return** changes. In particular,

   a) Compute fair present value if the required rate of return is 7%.
   b) What was the dollar change in value, from the value in problem 1?
   c) What was the percentage change in value, from the value in problem 1?
   d) Compute fair present value if the required rate of return is 13%.
   e) What was the dollar change in value, from the value in problem 1?
   f) What was the percentage change in value, from the value in problem 1?

3. Now, **THINK** about the calculations from the preceding question. Try to write down—in plain English—what you are observing.

For problems 4-6, consider a bond of Bonduel Corp., having the following characteristics—and note: except for **maturity**, the bond characteristics are just like those in *problem 1*.

Coupon rate:	8%
Payment frequency:	Semiannual
Maturity:	1 year
Par value:	$1,000
Required rate of return:	10%

4. Compute the bond's **fair present value.**

5. Compute the **fair present values, dollar value changes, and percentage value changes,** at required rates of **7%** and **13%.** In other words, follow parts (a) through (f) of problem 2—but applied to the Bonduel bond.

6. Now, look back at **problem 2** (parts c and f) **and problem 5** (parts c and f). These deal with the percentage change in value.

   a) Which bond shows the **biggest** percentage changes?
   b) Which bond would you guess has the largest **duration**? Note: You are *not* required to compute duration. Instead, *interpret* your answer to part (a).

7. In problems 1 and 4, the required rate of return is *higher* than the *coupon rate*. **Comment** on what would cause this.

For problems 8-10, consider the following bond:

Coupon rate:	12%
Payment frequency:	Annual
Maturity:	3 years
Par value:	$1,000
Current market price:	$ 950

8. Yield to maturity:
   a) **Set up** the equation that would be employed to find the bond's **yield to maturity.**
   b) With a business calculator or a spreadsheet program, **solve** for the **yield to maturity**.

9. Compute:
   a) the bond's **duration**. (Clue: you will need the yield to maturity from the preceding problem.)
   b) the bond's **modified duration.**

10. Let's suppose that this bond's yield to maturity increases by **two** percentage points.
    a) What happens to the bond's price? (Just in words—no computing yet.)
    b) Use your **duration** result (from above) to estimate the **new** price of the bond.
    c) Compute the bond's new price through present value techniques.
    d) Compare your answers from (b) and (c). Do they make sense?

11. A bond portfolio is valued at $210,000. Its yield to maturity is 8%, and its duration is 6.70. Now, suppose that market rates rise, so that the portfolio's yield to maturity goes to 9%. What would be the approximate **change** in the portfolio's value?

12. Consider a bond with *no* coupon payments. It will pay its own exactly $1,000 in three years. Right now, the bond is selling for $873. What is the duration of this bond?

III.   WASHING UP... AND THE "ABC" AWARDS

A. The EASIEST THING in the chapter

Well, it *should be* the **present value** of a bond. For example, getting the "fair present value" of the bonds in **Examples 3-1** and **3-2**. Granted, the present value formula applied to a bond can look messy. But it's a simple matter of "plug and chug." And, for those who have invested in a financial calculator or a spreadsheet program, it's *not a problem*.

B. The HARDEST THING in the chapter

The award goes to **duration**. The duration formula itself is a *real mess*. It can be a tedious calculation. But there's a good chance that duration will be computed *for you*— by a computer—in the real world. So, why call it "hard"? Because, for most of us, it's just *not obvious* that duration *really* tells us about the *sensitivity* of the bond value to interest rate changes. We have to do a bit of differential calculus to prove it—either that, or accept it on faith. And sometimes, even among the most devout, faith can waver.

C. The FUNNIEST THING in the chapter... or not

Take a look at the **In The News, 3-1,** from *The Wall Street Journal* of March 8, 2002. It's reported here that Mr. Greenspan, chairman of the Federal Reserve, made some rather modest changes in his economic outlook—and the bond market tanked. In particular, he had become a tad more optimistic about the economy. Hmm....why would *optimistic* comments have a negative impact on bond prices? Wouldn't a more robust economy mean greater better prospects for companies? Yes, it would. But better prospects would also suggest bigger demand for funds by businesses and consumers. (We can't forget that "loanable funds" stuff in Chapter 2, folks!) That, in turn, suggests upward pressure on interest rates. And just think about what happens when we discount future cash flows at a higher interest rate.

Hey, is Alan Greenspan a powerful guy, or what? Not only that, but he's getting some extra coverage even before his scheduled appearance in *our* textbook—heck, the Federal Reserve is covered in the *next* chapter! Wait your turn, Alan!

IV.   CHECKING THE ANSWERS...FOR SECTION II

Terms:
1. par bond
2. coupon rate
3. required rate of return
4. expected rate of return
5. market efficiency
6. convexity
7. yield to maturity
8. duration
9. modified duration
10. elasticity

Essay:
11. On fair present value and market efficiency:
    a) If the "fair present value" exceeds the going price, then investors would buy the security. They perceive it to be a "good deal." Their purchases would drive up the price, and eventually, it would equal the fair present value. Alternatively, if "fair present value" is less than the price, then investors would sell their holdings, driving down the price.
    b) In a highly efficient market, investors react quickly to unfairly priced securities. They buy or they sell, as suggested in the answer to part (a)—and the speed of their responses means that securities are not unfairly priced for long. If news travels more slowly, and investors are slow to respond, the market is *less* efficient.

Problems:
1. Simply apply the bond present value formula, as follows:

$$V_b = \frac{\$80}{2} \sum_{t=1}^{18} \left(\frac{1}{1 + .10/2} \right)^t + \frac{\$1,000}{[1+.10/2]^{18}} = \$883.10$$

Note that you are discounting a stream of 18 cash flows—*two* payments per year, for *nine* years.

2. Apply the same formula, but change the discount rate.

a) $V_b = \dfrac{\$80}{2} \displaystyle\sum_{t=1}^{18} \left(\dfrac{1}{1+.07/2} \right)^t + \dfrac{\$1,000}{[1+.07/2]^{18}} = \$1,065.95$

b) $1,065.95 minus $883.10, or an *increase* of $182.85.

c) The $182.85 represents a 20.7% increase.

d) $739.19

e) *Decrease* of $143.91

f) −16.3%

3. First, there is an inverse relationship between the fair price and the discount rate. Second, while we are taking the *same magnitude* of change in the discount rate— 3 percent—the resulting dollar (and percentage) changes in "fair price" are *not* identical. This demonstrates the "convex" nature of bond pricing.

4. Again, applying the present value formula:

$V_b = \dfrac{\$80}{2} \displaystyle\sum_{t=1}^{2} \left(\dfrac{1}{1+.10/2} \right)^t + \dfrac{\$1,000}{[1+.10/2]^2} = \$981.41$

5. It's present value time again:

a) $V_b = \dfrac{\$80}{2} \displaystyle\sum_{t=1}^{2} \left(\dfrac{1}{1+.07/2} \right)^t + \dfrac{\$1,000}{[1+.07/2]^2} = \$1,009.50$

b) A *dollar increase* of $28.09

c) $28.09 represents a 2.9% increase (from $981.41)

d) Now, putting .13 in as the discount rate, bond value = $954.48

e) A *dollar decrease* of $26.93

f) $26.93 represents a 2.7% decrease (from $981.41)

6. Comparing the two bonds:
   a) Bernice Corp.'s bond (problems 1-3) shows much greater percentage change than the Bonduel Corp.'s bond (problems 4 and 5)
   b) Bernice Corp.'s bond has the larger duration; this is suggested by the greater sensitivity of the bond to changes in interest rates.

7. The required rate of return (10%) exceeds the coupon rate (8%) because: (a) the market is demanding a higher return on bonds—i.e., market interest rates are higher than when the bond was new, and/or (b) the particular bond is perceived to be riskier.

8. For this 3-year bond:
   a) The 12% coupon rate means an annual coupon payment of $120. Put this, along with the bond price and face value, into the bond pricing equation. The *yield to maturity* is symbolized by the unknown discount rate (i).

$$\$950 = \$120 \sum_{t=1}^{3} \left(\frac{1}{1+i}\right)^t + \frac{\$1,000}{(1+i)^3}$$

   b) With a financial calculator, the yield to maturity is determined to be 14.16%. (Without a financial calculator or computer, finding the yield to maturity can be tedious—requiring "trial and error" to find the unknown discount rate.)

9. Follow the general formula below, which is for duration of a bond making *annual* payments. (With a semiannually paying bond, simply redefine the N, the CF, and the R so that they refer to six-month periods.)

$$D = \frac{\sum_{t=1}^{N} \frac{CF_t \times t}{(1+R)^t}}{\sum_{t=1}^{N} \frac{CF_t}{(1+R)^t}}$$

   a) Applying the formula to the bond of problem 8:

$$D = \frac{\left[\frac{\$120}{(1.1416)^1} \times 1\right] + \left[\frac{\$120}{(1.1416)^2} \times 2\right] + \left[\frac{\$1,120}{(1.1416)^3} \times 3\right]}{\frac{\$120}{(1.1416)^1} + \frac{\$120}{(1.1416)^2} + \frac{\$1,120}{(1.1416)^3}} = \frac{\$2,547.65}{\$950} = 2.682$$

Note that the denominator of the duration expression turns out to be the *price* of the bond. And that makes sense, because the denominator is simply expressing the present value of the bond's cash flows—and, given that we are using the yield to maturity as the discount rate, we will have to end up with the bond's price.

Also, note that the duration in this case—2.682—is *less* than the bond's maturity. This will always happen with a coupon-paying bond.

b) Modified duration is simply the duration divided by one plus the interest rate. Here:

$$MD = \frac{2.682}{(1+.1416)} = 2.349$$

10. Given the two percentage point increase in the YTM:
   a) The bond price must decrease.
   b) To estimate the new price, use the given information, and your computed yield to maturity, to solve for the change in price (dP). Remember that the duration can be interpreted as an elasticity:

$$\frac{\frac{dP}{P}}{\frac{dR}{(1+R)}} = -D \qquad \frac{\frac{dP}{\$950}}{\frac{+.02}{(1+.1416)}} = -2.682$$

dP = -44.64. So, the new bond price is estimated to be $950-$44.64, or $905.36

   c) Solving for price, using present value techniques, we discount the cash flows at a discount rate of 14.16% + 2.00% = 16.16%.

$$\$120\sum_{t=1}^{3}\left(\frac{1}{1+.1616}\right)^{t} + \frac{\$1,000}{(1+.1616)^{3}} = \$906.82$$

   d) The answer here is slightly larger than our conclusion based on duration. And that shouldn't be surprising. The duration-based procedure assumes that the relationship between price and yield to maturity is linear ("straight-line"). But in fact, it's a convex relationship.

11. Duration tells us about the elasticity:

$$\frac{\dfrac{dP}{P}}{\dfrac{dR}{(1+R)}} = -D$$

Here, instead of applying the formula to a single bond, we're applying it to a *portfolio*. The portfolio is initially valued at $210,000, so use that as P in the formula. The initial yield to maturity is 8%, so (1+R) is 1.08. The change in yield is 1%, or in decimal form, .01. Plugging in, we have the following:

$$\frac{\dfrac{dP}{\$210{,}000}}{\dfrac{.01}{(1+.08)}} = -6.70$$

Solving for the change in value, dP, we get $ -13,027.78. (Don't forget the "minus" sign!)

12. Well, you *can* do this in a rather *long* way. First, compute the security's yield to maturity. Then, plug into our "weighted average maturity" formula—the same thing that was employed in problem 9. But first, think about it. All of the cash inflow to the bond investor occurs at the maturity date. So, *all* the weight, in that weighted-average formula, has to be on the third and final cash flow. Bottom line: the duration has be exactly 3—identical to the bond's maturity.

CHAPTER 4
THE FEDERAL RESERVE SYSTEM, MONETARY POLICY, AND INTEREST RATES

I.   SURVEYING THE TERRITORY: AN AERIAL VIEW

Note the *last* thing in the chapter title: ***interest rates***. Haven't we visited this topic before? Absolutely. And very recently, in Chapter 3.

Interest rates are mighty important. And, as with lots of things in life, if something is really important, *somebody* will try to bottle it, package it, and yes, even *control it*. And if they can't control it, maybe they can at least "rein it in." And who is that *somebody*, in practice? Well, the generic term is the *central bank* of a nation.

In the U.S., the official public responsibility for influencing interest rates rests with the Federal Reserve System (or just the "Fed"). The Fed's been around since early in the 20th Century. So, it's had lots of time to learn, to evolve… and yes, it's probably made a few blunders along the way too. Chapter 4 tells us how it's *supposed* to work.

Back in Chapter 3, we learned that a supply and demand framework—for *loanable funds*—can be used to understand how interest rates are determined. You can look upon the Fed as influencing interest rates by affecting that supply-demand picture. The most obvious—and perhaps overly simplistic—way of viewing the Fed's impact is by recognizing it as a potential supplier of funds. But remember that there are lots of suppliers and demanders contributing to the overall interest rate outcome. And, it's worth noting that some very bright minds in the economics profession have argued long and hard on exactly *how* the Fed's actions are *transmitted* to the economy at large.

The chapter topic outline:

Major Duties and Responsibilities of the Federal Reserve System: Chapter Overview

Structure of the Federal Reserve System

Monetary Policy Tools

The Federal Reserve, the Money Supply, and Interest Rates

International Monetary Policies and Strategies

II.   DIGGING IN THE DIRT: A SUBTERRANEAN VIEW

Key terms

discount rate
discount window
check clearing
wire transfer
Federal Reserve Banks
Board of Governors
OCC
FDIC
FOMC
open market operations
reserves
monetary base
required reserves
excess reserves
fed funds rate
Federal Reserve Board Trading Desk
policy directive
repurchase agreement
the discount rate
adjustment credit
seasonal credit
extended credit
M1
M2
M3
foreign exchange intervention
Bank of Japan
European Central Bank
ECU

Got a question?

1. When the Federal Reserve engages in securities transactions—buying or selling government securities—with intentions of changing the money supply, influencing interest rates, and presumably, having a beneficial effect on various macroeconomic measures, it is conducting: _____.

2. When a commercial bank contacts its regional Federal Reserve Bank to borrow funds, we say that the bank is going to the: _____.

3. This decision-making body basically "calls the shots" in determining how the Fed's open market transactions will be conducted.
   This body is the: _____.

4. This group is physically part of the Federal Reserve Bank of New York. While it does not determine the Fed's monetary policy, it conducts the securities transactions that are intended to implement monetary policy.
   This is: _____.

5. The Federal Reserve Banks stand ready to lend money to depository institutions. The rate it charges borrowers is called the: _____.

6. A bank may choose to maintain reserves *above* the level required by the Federal Reserve.
   Such additional reserves are called: _____.

7. This a rate charged in "bank to bank" lending—when a depository lends excess reserves to another such institution.
   This is the: _____.

8. A bank borrows from the Federal Reserve, due to liquidity problems caused by *temporary* deposit outflows. This is the major type of discount loan from the Fed.
   This is referred to as: _____.

9. This is the aggregate of currency held by the public and reserves at depository institutions. Changes in this aggregate will lead to changes in the money supply.
   This aggregate is: _____.

10. When you write a check to pay a bill, the check must find its way back to your bank, *and* money from your bank account must find its way to the party who received your check.
    All this is referred to as: _____.

11. There are just *twelve* of these particular institutions. We might call them *banker's banks* in the U.S. banking framework. They are geographically dispersed, each within its own region, and have supervisory and regulatory responsibilities.
    These are: _____.

12. The _____ carries out central banking functions for not just one country, but a group of twelve.

13. In addition to the Federal Reserve, the _____ and the _____ serve important federal bank regulatory functions in the United States.

14. Explain, in general terms, what is happening as we go from M1 to M2 to M3. Also, what about the aggregate called "L"?

15. Suppose the Fed engineers an increase in the money supply.
    a) Explain, in general, what would happen to the level of interest rates and other economic indicators.
    b) Given your answer to part (a), speculate on subsequent effects on the demand for money.

Got a problem?

For problems 1-3, consider One-And-Only Bank (OAO). We'll assume it is the only bank in the economy, and it is subject to a 10% required reserve ratio, imposed by its central bank. Currently it has liabilities, in the form of transactions accounts, of $100 billion. It also has $10 billion in deposits on account with its central bank. Further, we assume that OAO wants to *just meet* the central bank's reserve requirement—so, it will always lend out any excess reserves.

1. Is OAO in compliance with the required reserve ratio?

2. What if: the central bank lowers the required reserve ratio to 8%. What impact would this have on transactions accounts in the economy?

3. What if: the central bank raises the required reserve ratio to 12%. What impact would this have on transactions accounts in the economy?

For problems 4-8, refer to the following: Trusty Bank's deposits are comprised of $300 billion in transactions accounts. It has a balance of $35 billion in its Federal Reserve Bank account. It has loans of $265 billion. The required reserve ratio (on transactions accounts) is 10%.

4. Compute Trusty Bank's level of **required reserves.**

5. Compute Trusty Bank's level of **excess reserves.**

6. Suppose now that Trusty Bank lends out all of its excess reserves. (And assume that any resulting, subsequent excess reserve amounts are also loaned out.) Compute the **change** in transactions deposits that would result from this action. (Clue: the text made a simplifying assumption for a problem like this: that there is *only one* bank in the system—Trusty Bank in this problem. You may make that same assumption, although it is not absolutely necessary if you interpret the resulting change in deposits as those occurring throughout the banking system.)

7. What would Trusty Bank's balance sheet now look like—if it happened to be the only bank in the system? (Ignore the things that obviously cannot be determined here: fixed assets, stockholders equity, etc.)

8. If the Federal Reserve happened to engage in an open market **purchase** of $25 billion, what would be the resulting **change** in **bank deposits**?

Web cruising ideas

For both of the exercises below, start by going the web site for the Federal Reserve's Board of Governors:

http://www.federalreserve.gov/

1. The beginning of Chapter 4 mentions the Humphrey-Hawkins Act, passed in 1978. Under the Act, the Federal Reserve must provide semiannual reports to Congress. Find the latest such report. (Clue: look for the topic "monetary policy.")

2. The Federal Open Market Committee meets regularly. After each meeting, the Committee releases a "statement," describing its intentions for the conduct of open market operations, as well as "minutes" for the meeting. Find the latest available statement and minutes. (Clue: look for the topic "monetary policy.")

III.   WASHING UP... AND THE "ABC" AWARDS

A.   The EASIEST THING in the chapter

The easiest thing is probably the information on the *structure* of the Federal Reserve System. We're talking "factual" here. Yes, it may be a little boring... but it's not hard.

B.   The HARDEST THING in the chapter

"Money supply or interest rates?" The Fed has at times targeted interest rates, but at other times, has shown more concern for the money supply numbers. (And, down through the years, there's been disagreement about exactly what the Fed *should* do.) Those who *really understand* the money supply material will understand *why* the Fed faces a *choice*—between using the money supply or the interest rate level as a target.

Let's suppose the Fed has decided to target the *money supply*. And, let's say it has determined that an open market purchase of $215 million is required. It enters the market, purchasing securities. The Fed has a pretty good idea about how its purchases will translate into money supply numbers. But, in contrast, it's hard to say exactly what the resulting effect will be on interest rate levels. Why? Well, there are *other* demanders and suppliers of funds. They have a *say* in this, through their transactions in the market. By deciding to purchase $215 million on the open market, the Fed is letting interest rates "find their own level."

On the other hand, suppose the Fed tries to target an interest rate level. How does it "push" the interest rate up or down? It buys or sells securities. But, by how much? The Fed probably has an idea about this—but it can be a fuzzy idea. So, the size of the open market operation is determined by "whatever is necessary" to achieve the desired interest rate. Therefore, the money supply change becomes the *result* of the Fed's attempt to achieve an interest rate target.

C.   The FUNNIEST THING in the chapter... or not

Hey, that money supply material is practically knee-slapping stuff, eh?

How would you like to have some of the chapter's topic—the money supply—for free? Huh? Well, aside from *controlling* the money supply, the regional Federal Reserve Banks also help *eliminate* the "unfit" currency from circulation. They shred the old money. And apparently, those wild and crazy characters at the Federal Reserve Banks have been known to distribute bags of *shredded* money, on request. Hmm... it might make a great stocking stuffer at Christmas time.

And you thought central bankers had no sense of humor.

IV. CHECKING THE ANSWERS...FOR SECTION II

Terms:
1. open market operations
2. discount window
3. Federal Open Market Committee
4. Federal Reserve Board Trading Desk
5. discount rate
6. excess reserves
7. fed funds rate
8. adjustment credit
9. the monetary base
10. check clearing
11. Federal Reserve Banks
12. European Central Bank
13. OCC and FDIC

Essays:
14. The "Ms" are different definitions of the money supply. Going to the "higher Ms" means that we are broadening our money definition. M1 includes items that can readily be used to conduct transactions—like currency, demand deposits, NOW accounts. But when we get to M3, we are including items that cannot be immediately be used for transactions—for example, large denomination CDs. The "L" aggregate is broader still. It includes M3, but also short-term Treasury securities, commercial paper, and bankers' acceptances.

15. When the Federal Reserve increases the money supply:
    a) It purchases securities, driving up bond prices and lowering bond yields—in other words, market interest rates fall. The lower interest rates may have an expansionary effect on the economy, stimulating production and expenditures. Increased employment may follow. Inflation is a possibility too.
    b) Given the expansionary effects described in part (a), the *demand* for money will probably increase—this would be depicted as a rightward shift in the money demand function (see the text's Figures 4-6 and 4-7). This can tend to "blunt" the lowering of the interest rate, as described in part (a). In fact, economists have argued about just how significant that money demand shift might be. The larger point here: while the Fed may have control over the money *supply*, all the rest of us can have big effect on the money *demand*. And both the *demand* and *supply* are important in interest rate determination. The Fed isn't determining interest rates *unilaterally*.

Problems:

1. Yes, the $10 billion held by OAO at its central bank is just 10% of the $100 billion of transactions account liabilities.

2. The lowering of the required reserve ratio will create excess reserves, which OAO can lend out. When all is said and done, OAO will make loans (thereby creating transactions deposits) up to the point where the $10 billion of reserves is just 8% of the new level of total transactions deposits. In particular: 8% × Transaction Deposits = $10 billion. The new level of transactions deposits will be $125 billion.

3. Here's a similar story, but with a crucially different outcome: 12% × Transaction Deposits = $10 billion. Transactions deposits will have to shrink to $83.33 billion. Faced with a higher reserve requirement, OAO will have to call in loans, or not renew existing loans.

4. Trusty Bank's *required reserves* would be 10 percent of $300 billion, or $30 billion.

5. Since Trusty is holding $35 billion at the Federal Reserve, it has an *excess reserve* of $35 billion less $30 billion, or $5 billion. (In a real world setting, it would also have some vault cash that would be counted as reserves—but, since the question makes no mention of this, we don't worry about it here.)

6. If Trusty lends out the $5 billion, then initially, it will create $5 billion in new deposits. But things don't stop there. Presumably, the *borrowers* will write checks on their new deposits. If Trusty is the only bank—obviously, an extreme assumption!—the checks come back to Trusty, and the reserves never leave Trusty. It lends again, but it lends somewhat less—because, with larger deposits, its excess reserves are somewhat less. The process would continue in this manner, until the deposit level is driven up to the point where Trusty's reserves ($35 billion) are *just* equal to its *required reserves*. This will occur when deposits equal $350 billion.

A shortcut: Take the amount of the excess reserves and simply *divide* by the required reserve ratio. This will quickly give you the *change* in deposits, or $50 billion.

Note: in reality, an individual bank like Trusty Bank would *not* be the only bank. So, checks written by borrowers would not always "come back" to Trusty. Even with many banks, however, the deposit expansion occurs in a very similar manner. But, with many banks, the resulting deposit increase is not isolated in just one institution. Instead, it is "distributed" among the many banks in the system.

7. Trusty Bank:

Assets		**Liabilities**	
Reserves	$35 billion	Transactions deposits	$350 billion
Loans	315 billion		

8. An open market purchase by the Fed would mean that the banking system (or just Trusty Bank, in a one-bank setting), would have additional excess reserves of $25 billion. Why are they "excess"? Reserves have increased, but deposits have not (at least not initially). The eventual increase in deposits would be $25 billion divided by the 10% required reserve ratio, or $250 billion.

CHAPTER 5
MONEY MARKETS

I.   SURVEYING THE TERRITORY: AN AERIAL VIEW

Looking over the chapter topics below, the dominant word is **money**. But don't get it mixed up with the *preceding* chapter's material. In Chapter 4, we also saw a lot of the "M-word," but we were talking about *pure liquidity* back there—the cash in the wallet, the balance in the checking account, etc.

Now, we're talking about markets for *short-term debt instruments*. If you want to get downright *literal* about things, Chapter 5 is really about stuff that's *close* to money. These assets will mature within a short time frame, and thereby *turn into* money. (And yes, my literal-reading friends, you might even prefer to call these the **"*close to* money markets"**—but don't tell anybody I said it was OK.)

Summary of chapter topics:

Definition of Money Markets: Chapter Overview

Money Markets

Money Market Securities

Money Market Participants

International Aspects of Money Markets

Euro Money Markets

**Appendix: Single versus Discriminating Price Treasury Auctions
(available at www.mhhe.com/sc2e)**

Note that the very last topic appears in an appendix—which is available at the textbook's web site.

II.   DIGGING IN THE DIRT: A SUBTERRANEAN VIEW

Key terms

    money market
    opportunity cost
    default risk
    Treasury bills
    Treasury bill auction
    competitive bid
    noncompetitive bid
    fed funds
    federal funds rate
    federal funds purchased
    federal funds sold
    correspondent banks
    repurchase agreement
    reverse repurchase agreement
    commercial paper
    negotiable certificate of deposit
    bearer instrument
    banker's acceptance
    Eurodollar deposits
    Eurodollar market
    LIBOR
    Eurodollar floating rate CD
    Euronotes
    Eurocommercial paper

Got a question?

1. A bank typically has reciprocal accounts and agreements with other banks. And it may borrow from, or lend to, such other banks.
    Banks in such a relationship are called: _____.

2. An institution places a bid in the auction for 26-week Treasury bills. The institution *may* receive bills, or *may not*—it depends on how its bid price matches up against the prices of other bidders.
    This institution is participating in the _____ part of the auction.

3. A bank agrees to **lend** excess reserves to another bank. As a result, this bank will have an account entitled _____ among its assets.

4. Look again at the transaction in the preceding question, but change perspective.
    The bank **borrowing** the reserves will have an account entitled _____ among its liabilities.

5. Institution X **buys** securities from Institution Y, and simultaneously promises to **sell** them back—at a specified later time, and for a specified price. From the perspective of Institution X, this is a: _____.

6. Look again at the transaction in the preceding question, but change perspective. Viewed from the perspective of the Institution Y—the one who originally **sells**, while promising to **buy back** later—this is a: _____.

7. A _____ is a time draft payable to a seller of goods, with payment guaranteed by a bank.

8. _____ are the most actively traded of the money market securities.

9. An inter-bank market for overnight, Eurodollar funds is based in London. The rate charged in this market is called: _____.

10. Dollar-denominated deposits held outside the U.S.—by overseas branches of U.S. banks or other banks—are called _____.

11. The market for securities having an original maturity of up to one year is called the: _____.

12. _____ is a short-term promissory note issued by a corporation, to raise short-term cash.

13. _____ refers to the risk of late payment, or non-payment.

14. What are the two key differences between the **discount yield** and **bond equivalent yield**? Given these differences, what can we say about the *relationship* between these yields, when applied to the same securities?

15. What has been the relationship between LIBOR rates and federal funds (U.S.) rates? Why?

16. With respect to commercial paper in the U.S.:
    a) What are the maturities for such securities?
    b) How does the secondary market activity for commercial paper compare with that for U.S. Treasury bills?

Got a problem?

1. A Treasury bill, with face value of $10,000, has 91 days to maturity. Jerry just paid $9,812 for it.
   a) Calculate the "discount yield" on the T-bill.
   b) Calculate the "bond equivalent yield" on the T-bill.

2. A Treasury bill, with face value of $10,000, has a discount yield of 3.20%. It has 34 days to maturity. What is its price?

3. A Treasury bill, with face value of $10,000, has a bond equivalent yield of 4.60%. It has 60 days to maturity. What is its price?

4. Teresa is looking at Treasury bill data from yesterday's *Wall Street Journal*. She observes an **"asked" discount yield** of 6.58%, on T-bills with 124 days left to maturity.

   a) What would the **asked price** have been, assuming a T-bill quantity of $100,000 face value?
   b) What is the meaning of the **asked price**?
   c) What would the **bond equivalent yield** have been, based on the **asked** price?

5. Student Pleasers, Inc. issues $5 million (face value) in commercial paper, at a **discount yield** of 7.80%. The maturity is 270 days.
   a) Compute the price paid by investors for the paper.
   b) Compute the **bond equivalent yield** on the paper.

Web cruising ideas

1. Want to see the **Treasury Direct** setup? And see it downright *directly*? Well, poke around at the following site, for the Bureau of Public Debt:

   http://www.publicdebt.treas.gov/

2. Okay, let's see if you can find the Treasury's auction calendar—that is, the upcoming schedule for offerings of new securities. Go to the web site just listed, and search around for "auction."

3. We're having so much fun with the Treasury, why stop now? Stick with the same site, but now try to locate the latest news release, containing the most recent **auction results**. Let's say we're looking for the 13-week T-bill results. Think "Public Debt News" as you browse the site, and you should have no trouble. When you find it, note two things: (1) there's a much larger dollar volume in the *competitive bid* part of the auction, and (2) *all* of the *noncompetitive bid* orders are filled—in stark contrast to the competitive segment.

III.   WASHING UP... AND THE "ABC" AWARDS

A. The EASIEST THING in the chapter

Well, once you've got it down, the **discount yield** and **bond equivalent yield** should get the honors here.

B. The HARDEST THING in the chapter

The instruments in the international sphere can be hard to distinguish, at least for those of us who aren't straddling international borders on a regular basis.

C. The FUNNIEST THING in the chapter... or not

As usual, we don't have huge laughs here, but here are a couple of things. First, how about some ammunition for your next trivia contest? Like: How much did the Bureau of Public Debt receive in *gifts* in 2002? That's right, I said *gifts*—for the purpose of reducing the public debt. Some loyal patriots actually *give* money to the government! Ready for the answer? In the year 2002, it came to $744,675.06. And you can find instructions for making *your* gift at the web site listed previously.

One other interesting note: I came across the Treasury Department's "Recreation Association," and more to the point, its *gift shop*! Soon I found myself in a virtual department store of merchandise... all with the U.S. Treasury's logo! You can buy jewelry, golf shirts, and heck, probably even golf balls. Why you would want to become a walking billboard for the U.S. Treasury is beyond me. But, on second thought, who knows... perhaps there are *some* golf courses where the Treasury logo is good for a preferred tee-off time. *"Sir, we're from the U.S. Treasury, and our top-secret surveillance activities have brought us to your golf course...could we get on the course immediately?"* Oh yeah... if you're interested, go to:

https://studioenterprises.securelook.com/

IV.   CHECKING THE ANSWERS...FOR SECTION II

Terms:
1. correspondent banks
2. competitive bid
3. federal funds sold
4. federal funds purchased
5. reverse repurchase agreement
6. repurchase agreement
7. banker's acceptance
8. Treasury bills
9. LIBOR (or London Interbank Offered Rate)
10. Eurodollar deposits
11. money market
12. commercial paper
13. default risk

Essays:
14. First, the *discount yield* divides the dollars earned by the face or par value of the T-bills, while the *bond equivalent yield* divides by the amount *paid* for the bills. The bond equivalent methodology is a more "intuitively comfortable" method—since we are dividing by the amount invested. Second, the *discount yield* multiplies by 360 days, while the *bond equivalent yield* multiplies by 365. It's as if the bank discount yield is assuming there are twelve 30-day months in a year.

    The discount yield is dividing by a *bigger* number and multiplying by a *smaller* number—in comparison with the bond equivalent yield. So, when applied to the same T-bills, the discount yield will always be *smaller* than the bond equivalent yield.

15. The LIBOR rate has been somewhat higher than the fed funds rate in the U.S. (See the text's Figure 5-10). Both of these rates apply to very short-term, bank-to-bank transactions. The reason for the difference is rooted in perceived risk differences between U.S. and overseas banks. Aside from the explicit government deposit insurance, which is relevant for a large portion of U.S. bank deposits, there may be an "implicit" government guarantee—the perception that large U.S. banks would be supported by regulator actions in times of trouble.

16. Commercial paper:
    a) Commercial paper is issued for maturities up to 270 days, although the most common maturities are from 20 to 45 days. The 270-day figure results from SEC registration requirements that would apply if the maturity were longer.
    b) There is an active secondary market for T-bills, but there is little secondary market activity for commercial paper.

Problems:

1. For the 91-day T-bills:

   a) $$\frac{\$10{,}000 - \$9{,}812}{\$10{,}000} \times \frac{360}{91} = .0743 = 7.43\%$$

   b) $$\frac{\$10{,}000 - \$9{,}812}{\$9{,}812} \times \frac{365}{91} = .0769 = 7.69\%$$

2. Use the same type of equation as in problem 1(a), but now the price is the unknown. So,

   $$\frac{\$10{,}000 - P}{\$10{,}000} \times \frac{360}{34} = .032$$

   A little algebra will give you P = $9,969.78.

3. Now use the same type of equation as in problem 1(b), but treating the price as the unknown.

   $$\frac{\$10{,}000 - P}{P} \times \frac{365}{60} = .046$$

   The algebra's a tiny bit harder this time, because P appears in two places. Below is a helpful first step, to get you going.

   $$\left(\frac{\$10{,}000}{P} - \frac{P}{P} \right) \times \frac{365}{60} = .046$$

   Of course, the P/P term is simply equal to 1. Now solve for the remaining P, which is $9,924.95.

4. For the 124-day T-bills:

   a) We need to solve the following equation:
   $$\frac{\$100{,}000 - P_0}{\$100{,}000} \times \frac{360}{124} = .0658$$

   Solving for P_0, we get $97,733.56

b) The asked price corresponds to the price asked by the securities dealer—or, the amount paid by the investor.

c) Apply the bond equivalent yield formula, given the price from part (a):

$$\frac{\$100,000 - \$97,733.56}{\$97,733.56} \times \frac{365}{124} = .0683 = 6.83\%$$

5. This can be handled analogously to the T-bill calculations.

a) $$\frac{\$5,000,000 - P_0}{\$5,000,000} \times \frac{360}{270} = .0780$$

Solving for the unknown price, we get $P_0 = \$4,707,500$

b) Now, use the price from part (a) in the bond equivalent formula.

$$\frac{\$5,000,000 - \$4,707,500}{\$4,707,500} \times \frac{365}{270} = .0840$$

CHAPTER 6
BOND MARKETS

I. SURVEYING THE TERRITORY: AN AERIAL VIEW

Bonds markets comprise one segment of the **capital markets**—i.e., the market for longer-term instruments, with maturities beyond one year. With bonds, we are dealing with longer-term *borrowing* agreements. The *borrower* (perhaps a company, perhaps a governmental unit) issues the bond, which is purchased by a *lender*. And there may well be a number of such lenders. One lender might be a pension fund, while another could be an individual, purchasing bonds for her own account. We usually call these lenders *investors*. After the initial sale, the bonds can change hands in secondary market transactions.

The bond issue can take on various structures. A very common one is for the issuer to promise fixed interest payments on a regular, periodic basis, and then to return the amount borrowed at maturity. This is the essence of a fixed rate, coupon bond. But we could also have a structure with no coupon payments at all. And there are even more complicated structures—such as bonds that are *convertible*. (No, you can't put the top down.)

By the way, contrast *bonds* with another kind of borrowing agreement: a *bank loan*. Traditionally—and even today, for many loans—*one* bank plays the role of lender. And traditionally, that one bank would hold onto the loan. But now, it is commonplace to see many loans "packaged" together. Claims on the package can be sold to a number of investors. As a result, the loans start to look very "bond-like." You'll hear more about this in Chapter 7 (Mortgage Markets) and Chapter 10 (Derivative Markets). The bottom line: bonds used to be distinctly different from bank loans. And yes, they *still are* different. But the differences are much fuzzier now.

Chapter topics:

Definition of Bond Markets: Chapter Overview

Bond Market Securities

Bond Market Participants

Comparison of Bond Market Securities

International Aspects of Bond Markets

Eurobonds, Foreign Bonds, and Brady and Sovereign Bonds

II. DIGGING IN THE DIRT: A SUBTERRANEAN VIEW

Key terms

capital markets	bearer bond
bonds	registered bond
bond markets	term bond
T-notes	serial bond
T-bonds	crisis at maturity
STRIP	mortgage bond
dirty price	debenture
clean price	subordinated debenture
accrued interest	convertible bond
municipal bonds	stock warrant
general obligation bonds	call provision
revenue bonds	call premium
IDB	sinking fund provision
firm commitment underwriting	junk bond
best efforts underwriting	Eurobond
private placement	foreign bond
corporate bonds	Brady bond
bond indenture	sovereign bond

Got a question?

1. A bond purchaser must compensate the seller for interest *earned by the seller*, but *not yet received* by the seller. You can view the amount as a portion of the upcoming coupon payment—the portion earned as of the time the bond sale is settled.
   This amount is called: _____.

2. Suppose an investment bank agrees to sell a company's new debt, but it does *not* guarantee a price to the issuer. The investment banker receives a fee for distributing the issue.
   This is called a: _____.

3. This is an unsecured bond, but in addition, it is in a *junior* position. As such, it is a riskier type of bond.
   This is called a: _____.

4. Sometimes, a bond issue contains many different maturity dates. A portion of the bond issue is thus paid off on each date.
   This is a: _____.

5. This term is an acronym, with two of its letters standing for "interest" and "principal."
   The term is: _____.

6. A _____ is one rated as "less than investment grade" by bond-rating agencies.

7. A number of bank loans made to borrowers in emerging market countries have been converted into bonds—with longer maturities and lower coupon rates than the original debts. The loans have been "consolidated" at the various central banks of the emerging market countries.
A bond created in this way is a: _____.

8. The interest payments made by _____ are exempt from federal income taxes.

9. A _____ is a type of municipal bond used to finance a specific, revenue-generating project. Revenue from the project is used to pay of this type of bond.

10. Some bonds indentures include a plan for periodic redemption of the bonds. At predetermined intervals, the issuing firm buys back outstanding bonds from a portion of the bondholder group.
Such bonds are said to have a: _____.

11. A/an _____ is a type of bond issued by municipalities on behalf of a corporation, to help build the economic base of the municipality.

12. A bond buyer must pay a price including accrued interest. This full price is also known as the _____.

13. Some bond issuers prefer to have their principal payments extended over a longer period, rather than coming due at one time.
This helps to avoid a _____.

14. Suppose a financial institution "strips" a 30-year Treasury bond. How many new, separately-traded securities are created? Further, describe the nature of the newly created securities—what aspects make them different from the 30-year Treasury bond?

15. Explain the risk faced by an investment bank when it engages in "firm commitment underwriting."

16. Explain a "call provision." Further, how do changes in market interest rates influence the "exercise" of such a provision?

17. A firm is contemplating having a "convertibility" feature attached to a new bond issue. In general, how would this affect the yield on the bond? Higher yield? Lower? Explain.

Got a problem?

1. A Treasury note has been "stripped." It has a 9% coupon rate, a face value of $10,000, and exactly 5 years to maturity. And, the first coupon payment will occur exactly 6 months from now. The current **yield to maturity** on the T-note is 9.20%.
   a) Compute the **present value**, or **price** of the T-note.
   b) Compute the **present value** of the **fourth** coupon payment.

2. A Treasury bond is listed in *The Wall Street Journal* at a price of 103:26. What does this mean—in terms of the actual price?

3. The "asked" price on a Treasury strip is currently listed as 80:00 (or exactly 80% of face value). The maturity is exactly 4 years. Calculate the **yield to maturity** on this strip. (Clue: set it up using the "semiannual compounding" assumption, even though there is only one payment, at maturity.)

4. A T-bond has a 6.80% coupon rate. Its face value is $10,000. The bond is being sold. The settlement date is 75 days since the most recent coupon payment. At settlement, there will be 107 days until the next coupon payment. Compute the amount of the **accrued interest** on the bond.

5. On January 13, 2003, Stan purchases a $10,000 T-note that matures on November 15, 2008. (Settlement for occurs two days after purchase, on January 15.) The coupon rate is 4.75%. The *clean* price quote at the time of Stan's purchase is 106:31.
   a) What **accrued interest** must Stan pay?
   b) What is the full, actual price Stan must pay?
   c) What is the **yield to maturity** on the note?

6. A municipal bond offers an interest rate of 6%. Lana's marginal Federal tax rate is 28%. For Lana, what rate on a corporate bond would be **equivalent** the rate on the municipal (ignoring default risk considerations)?

Web cruising ideas

1. We've mentioned the Treasury Department's web site before, but you might also be interested in a private site, sponsored by The Bond Market Association. You'll see their take on the latest "legislative" and "regulatory" issues, as well as information on the markets. There are also links to other bond-related information.

   http://www.bondmarkets.com/

2. Once you're at The Bond Market Association's site, see if you can find a table, presenting estimates of who exactly is holding the public debt in the U.S. (Clue: Try looking under *Research* and *Statistics*.)

3. If you're interested in credit ratings, try S&P's site. (You will probably be asked to go through a free registration process, to gain access.)

    http://www2.standardandpoors.com/NASApp/cs/ContentServer?pagename=sp/Page/HomePg

III. WASHING UP… AND THE "ABC" AWARDS

A. The EASIEST THING in the chapter

Taking the present value of a Treasury STRIP. (Well, that's assuming we're not quibbling about the "right" discount rate to use!) But seriously, a zero coupon instrument provides the easiest present value problem imaginable.

B. The HARDEST THING in the chapter

Let's call it "keeping the players straight without a scorecard." You may reach a virtual **memory overload**, when the topic is *types of bonds*. (For professors writing exams, this chapter provides a "gold mine" of terms, tailor-made to trip up students.)

C. The FUNNIEST THING in the chapter… or not

This isn't funny, just peculiar. It's a thorny terminology thing, relating to *Euro*-stuff. What am I getting at? Well, a **Eurobond** *could* have *little or nothing* to do with Europe! Eurobonds are simply bonds sold beyond the borders of the country in which they are denominated. So, let's say a U.S. firm sells dollar-denominated bonds in Japan. It's a Eurobond. Why? Well, it probably results from our human tendency to take a **specific** term and apply it to a more **general** class—just as I might ask for "Coke" when ordering a "cola."

IV. CHECKING THE ANSWERS…FOR SECTION II

Terms:
1. accrued interest
2. best efforts underwriting
3. subordinated debenture
4. serial bond
5. STRIP
6. junk bond
7. Brady bond

8. municipal bonds (which also include general obligation and revenue bonds)
9. revenue bond
10. sinking fund provision
11. IDB
12. dirty price
13. crisis at maturity

Essays:

14. There would be 61 claims created from the 30-year Treasury bond. The 30-year bond has 60 semiannual coupon payments, one every six months. Then, at maturity, there is the repayment of the face value. The 61 claims are different from the original T-bond in that they are all *zero coupon* securities. Also, they have various maturities, up to 30 years.

15. When doing a firm commitment underwriting, the investment bankers are promising a certain amount to the issuer of the securities. There is always a chance that the investment bankers cannot sell the issue as expected. Market conditions could change after they have made their commitment, or perhaps new, negative information about the issuer becomes available—in such a case, the investment bankers would have to "chisel down" the price, and their expected profit on the deal will fall.

16. When a bond has a call provision, the issuer—i.e., the borrower of the funds—has the right to buy the bonds back from investors. And, the buy-back price, or "call price" is known—it is specified in the bond's call provision. When would an issuer want to call in an issue? Well, think about interest rates. If interest rates have fallen since the bond's issuance, the borrowing firm can save interest expenses by calling in the bonds, and issuing new bonds with the lower interest rate. What might cause rates to fall in the first place? It could simply be a change in general market conditions, or it could be that the borrower's credit status is improving. In contrast, if interest rates have risen since the bonds were issued, a call is less likely.

17. An example of a "convertibility" feature would be a bond that can be converted into the issuing firm's stock. A convertible bond gives the investor an option to do something in the future. The conversion option is valuable. So, investors will be willing to pay relatively more for a bond with such a feature (keeping "other things equal," of course). And if investors pay relatively *more*, then the bond's yield will be *less*. In fact, viewed from the issuer's perspective, attaching a convertibility feature to a bond might be a way of reducing interest expense.

Problems:

1. Simply take the present value of the note's cash flows, using the yield to maturity as the discount rate.

a) $V_b = \dfrac{\$900}{2} \displaystyle\sum_{t=1}^{10} \left(\dfrac{1}{1+.092/2} \right)^t + \dfrac{\$10,000}{[1+.092/2]^{18}} = \$9,921.26$

b) The fourth coupon payment would be received exactly two years in the future. Discount that one payment back to present value.

$$V = \dfrac{\$450}{\left(1+.092/2\right)^4} = \$375.91$$

Note that we have used the yield to maturity as the discount rate—with the given information, it is the only possible choice. But, it is possible that valuing *different* coupon payments would require *different* discount rates (basically, this is due to the different maturities represented among the various cash flows of the bond). The sum of the present values of all the individual cash flows should equal the value of the bond, however.

2. This number should be interpreted as a percentage of the bond's face value. Further, the number to the right of the colon (:) is in 32nds. So, 103:26 means 103.8125 percent of the face value. (Note that 26/32 equals 0.08125.) One final thing: this is known as a *clean* price—meaning it does not take into account any *accrued interest* since the most recent coupon payment. The buy would have to pay the clean price *plus* the accrued interest.

3. The strip is a zero coupon instrument. So, set up a present value equation; the yield to maturity (ytm) is the discount rate that makes the equation true.

$$80\% = \dfrac{100\%}{\left(1 + ytm/2\right)^8}$$

Solving this, ytm = .0566 or 5.66%

4. This one's a pain—no doubt about it! The pain has to do with the seemingly "small matters" of getting the correct number of days. First, note that coupon payments will occur on November 15 and May 15 (Why May 15th? Because notes pay semiannually.) Also note that Stan's settlement date will be on January 15—which is 61 days since the last coupon payment, on November 15. Now, how many days are in the current coupon period—from November 15 through May 15? It comes to 181 (which may seem low, but February is in there).
   a) Accrued interest:

$$\dfrac{4.75\%}{2} \times \$10,000 \times \dfrac{61}{181} = \$80.04$$

b) Find the *clean price* and add in the accrued interest from part a. The clean price is quoted at 106:31. Remember, the right side of the colon is in 32nds. So, the dollar amount, based on this *clean* quote is:

$$106.96875\% \times \$10{,}000 = \$10{,}696.88$$

Add the accrued interest to this, getting a full price of $10,776.92.

c) The yield to maturity is based on the clean quote. As earlier, a little extra pain is related to the exact time to maturity. Earlier, we said that Stan's settlement date is 61 days from the last coupon, on November 15. So, there must be 365-61, or 304 days until the bond's "anniversary date" (no, don't worry about sending flowers—but it was a nice thought). You need to set up the bond's present value equation for a period of 5 years and a fraction—the fraction being 304/365, or 0.8329.

The folks using financial calculators have a *super-serious* advantage in getting yields to maturity on problems like this one (without one, we're talking long, long nights of "trial and error").

Below is the set-up.

$$106.96875\% = \frac{4.75\%}{2}\left(PVIFA_{?\!\!/\!2\,,\,5.8329\times2}\right) + 100\%\left(PVIF_{?\!\!/\!2\,,\,5.8329\times2}\right)$$

The left-hand side is the bond's price, expressed as a percentage of face value. The right-hand side contains, first the present value of all the coupons, and second, the present value of the face (again, everything is being expressed as a percent of face value). You're looking for the question mark—in other words, the discount rate that will force the bond's clean price (106.96875%) to equal the present value of all the cash flows. There are 5.8329 years until maturity—or *(5.829 times 2)* six-month periods. And now...drum roll... the answer please! It's **3.42%.** (If you do not have a financial calculator, see if you can use this answer to *verify* the formula above.)

5. The semiannual coupon payment is (.068/2) times $10,000, or $340. There are a total of 107 + 75 =182 days in the interval between the most recent coupon payment and the upcoming one. The accrued interest is based on the fraction of the upcoming coupon payment that has been *earned*.

So, the accrued interest $= \dfrac{107}{182} \times \$340 = \$199.89$

6. Set the after-tax rate on the *taxable bond* equal to the *municipal bond rate*, and then solve for the pre-tax bond rate.

Given Lana's 28% tax rate, we have:

After-tax rate on taxable bond = municipal bond rate

(1-.28)(taxable bond rate, pre-tax) = municipal bond rate

(1-.28)(taxable bond rate, pre-tax) = 6%

Solving, the taxable bond rate, pre-tax = 8.33%

CHAPTER 7
MORTGAGE MARKETS

I. SURVEYING THE TERRITORY: AN AERIAL VIEW

This chapter, like Chapter 6, deals with *debt* agreements. But the distinguishing feature here is *real estate*, which is serving as *collateral* for the debt. Most readers will have some familiarity with a mortgage loan. But the variety of loan and bond types having real estate as collateral is enough to boggle the mind. Someone (or maybe a *bunch* of "someones") figured out two important things: (a) that the folks who *make* the loans might not always want to *keep* the loans, and (b) that investors might have different needs—so we might see investors interested in a variety of different claims against mortgage portfolios. If you're looking for creativity in the world of finance, you'll find it in the mortgage area.

The chapter outline:

Mortgages and Mortgage-backed Securities: Chapter Overview

Primary Mortgage Market

Secondary Mortgage Markets

Participants in the Mortgage Markets

International Trends in Securitization

II. DIGGING IN THE DIRT: A SUBTERRANEAN VIEW

Key terms

> **mortgage**
> **securitized**
> **collateral**
> **lien**
> **down payment**
> **private mortgage insurance (PMI)**
> **federally insured mortgage**
> **conventional mortgage**
> **amortized**
> **balloon payment mortgage**
> **fixed rate mortgage**
> **adjustable rate mortgage (ARM)**
> **discount points**
> **mortgage refinancing**

amortization schedule
automatic rate-reduction mortgage
graduated payment mortgage (GPM)
growing-equity mortgage (GEM)
second mortgage
home equity loan
shared-appreciation mortgage (SAM)
equity-participation mortgage (EPM)
reverse-annuity mortgage (RAM)
correspondent banking
participation
mortgage sale
recourse
securitization
pass-through mortgage securities
timing insurance
Ginnie Mae
Fannie Mae
Freddie Mac
FHA
VA
FMHA
collateralized mortgage obligation (CMO)
tranches
mortgage pass-through strip
REMIC
IO strip
PO strip
mortgage-backed bond (MBB)

Got a question?

1. The Federal National Mortgage Association was created in 1938. It purchases packages of mortgage loans, financing such purchases by selling mortgage-backed securities to investors.
   This agency is known as: _____.

2. When mortgages are packaged and sold as assets backing a publicly traded or privately held debt instrument, we say they are: _____.

3. _____ are fees or payments made when a mortgage loan is issued. They are quoted as a percentage of the principal value of the mortgage.

4. The _____ shows how the a loan's various payments are split between interest and principal.

5. A _____ is a public record attached to the title of a property, allowing the lender to sell the property if the borrower defaults.

6. A lending institution or third-party servicer receives the principal and interest payments from mortgage borrowers, but then sends pro rate shares of the payments to various investors.
   The investors in this scenario are holders of: _____.

7. The _____ is a vehicle for securitizing loans. It is a type of mortgage-backed bond having a number of different classes, with each class having a different guaranteed coupon.

8. With a _____, the mortgage borrower *receives* regular payments from the financial institution rather than making them. Upon maturity (or the borrower's death), the property is sold to retire the debt.

9. With a _____, the mortgage borrower agrees that, if the financed property is eventually sold at a gain, the lender will receive part of the gain. The home buyer can obtain a lower interest rate in return.

10. This type of mortgage allows borrowers to make smaller payments early-on, and then face increased payments later. The expectation is that the borrower's income will be rising over time, so a larger amount can be financed.
    This is the: _____.

11. Sometimes a mortgage loan entails a borrower's purchase of an associated insurance contract. In the event of a loan default, and sale of the mortgaged property, the insurance company will compensate the lender if the sale proceeds do not cover the outstanding loan balance.
    This is: _____ ____.

12. A _____ requires a fixed monthly interest payment (and sometimes, principal payments) for a three to five year period. Then the full remaining balance is due.

13. The various classes of a collateralized mortgage obligation arrangement are called: _____.

14. A provision in the 1986 Tax Reform Act authorized the creation of a new type of mortgage-backed security called a _____, which allows for the pass-through of all interest and principal payments before taxes are levied.

15. _____ describes the situation wherein a mortgage borrower takes out a new mortgage and uses the proceeds to pay off an existing mortgage.

63

16. Ginnie Mae supports pools of mortgage loans whose default risk is insured by
_____, _____, or _____.

17. Distinguish a loan sale **with recourse** from one **without recourse**. Also, what would be the yield or return consequences of these two types of sale?

18. From an investor's perspective, how does a CMO investment differ from a pass-through investment?

19. What are key things that distinguish **mortgage backed bonds** from **pass-throughs** and **CMOs**?

20. **IO strip** will behave differently than a **PO strip** as market interest rates change. Why?

Got a problem?

1. Sue borrows $110,000 to finance a home purchase. The loan has a fixed interest rate of 9%, and the monthly payments will be fully amortizing over 15 years. Compute the amount of Sue's **monthly payment**.

2. Referring to the preceding problem, compute the following, for each of the **first two** loan payments:
   a) the amount of **interest** in the payment
   b) the amount of **principal** paid in the payment
   c) the **balance due** on the loan, immediately after the payment. (Clue: financial calculators and spreadsheet programs will have a pre-programmed features that can be used for this problem—but it can be good to try it "by hand," at least for the first payment. Then, compare with the calculator solution.)

3. Still referring to problem 1, what if the loan amount and interest rate were the same, but the loan were amortized over **30 years**?
   a) Compute the amount of the **loan payment**.
   b) How mush **total amount of interest** would Sue pay, over the entire **30-year** life of the loan?
   c) Compare your answer to (b) with the **total amount of interest** that would be paid with the **15-year** life of the loan in problem 1.

4. Bernard applies for a 30-year mortgage loan in the amount of $170,000. The lending institution quotes him two alternatives: (1) a loan with no points, to be paid off in monthly installments at an interest rate of 6.00%, or (2) a loan with 1.5 points, to be paid off in monthly installments at an interest rate of 5.75%.
   a) What is the monthly payment on option (1)—with no points?
   b) What is the monthly payment on option (2)—with 1.5 points?
   c) Determine the present value of the points—evaluated at the interest rate of 5.75%. How does this compare with the dollar amount of points being charged by the lender?

5. Tina has applied for a mortgage loan in the amount of $90,000. The lending institution offers the following: A five year mortgage loan, at 8%, with five years of fixed monthly payments, and a balloon payment due at the end of five years. The monthly payments will be based on a 30-year amortization schedule.
   a) What is the monthly payment?
   b) What is the amount of the balloon payment?
   c) How much interest would Tina pay over the five year life of this loan?

Web cruising ideas

Freddie Mac's web site has some interesting stuff. Here are two examples:

1. The following site takes you to the Freddie Mac web site—in particular, to a page linking you to issues of a relatively new Freddie Mac publication, *Gold Perspective*. Some interesting stuff, for mortgage market mavens.

   http://www.freddiemac.com/mbs/html/bul_main.html

2. Freddie also publishes results of its "primary mortgage market survey," which provides current market interest rate data—including 15-year, 30-year, and ARM products.

   http://www.freddiemac.com/pmms/

III. WASHING UP... AND THE "ABC" AWARDS

A. The EASIEST THING in the chapter

Given that "time value of money" calculations were covered earlier in the text, the exercise of computing a loan payment *should* be a snap. (Of course, what *should be* may differ from what *is*.)

B. The HARDEST THING in the chapter

There's a lot of material on CMOs, IOs, POs, and the like—and it can be difficult to keep it all straight. But if you have trouble with the detail, try at least to understand the broader picture.

C. The FUNNIEST THING in the chapter... or not

How about one thing *in the chapter* and one thing *out*?

The *"out"* stuff first: Visit an archive at Freddie Mac's web site, providing access to a publication called *SMM* (for Secondary Mortgage Markets). You'll see an article from December 1999 entitled "Who Pays, Who Strays, and Who Delays." Here's the link:

> http://www.freddiemac.com/finance/smm/current.htm

One little interesting tidbit there is on *skip-tracers*. Meaning? Well, we all know that in troubled times, some borrowers start skipping... as in *skipping* out on their obligations. You'll find some skip-tracing ideas here.

Now, right there, *"in"* the chapter: Take a look at Figure 7-11, and what do *you* see? It's supposed to relate to mortgages. But I see a fish. (Guess I should have majored in ichthyology.)

IV.   CHECKING THE ANSWERS...FOR SECTION II

Terms:
1. Fannie Mae
2. securitized
3. discount points
4. amortization schedule
5. lien
6. pass-through mortgage securities (although there are some other, more specific pass-through terms in our list)
7. collateralized mortgage obligation (CMO)
8. reverse-annuity mortgage (RAM)
9. shared-appreciation mortgage (SAM)
10. graduated-payment mortgage (GPM)
11. private mortgage insurance (PMI)
12. balloon payment mortgage
13. tranches
14. REMIC
15. mortgage refinancing
16. FHA (Federal Housing Administration), VA (Veterans Administration), or FMHA (Farmers Home Administration)

Essays:
17. When an institution sells loans *without recourse*, then the buyer is assuming all of the credit risk inherent in the loans. If the loans are sold *with recourse*, then the seller, under certain conditions, is contingently liable if the loans go bad. The buyer of loans *without* recourse would be taking on more risk, and consequently, we would expect such a buyer to receive relatively more return—in compensation for that risk.

18. An investor in a pass-through has a claim against a package of mortgages, and will receive a pro rate share of the principal and interest payments being made by borrowers. Payments are "passed through" as they are received by the lender or loan servicer Consequently, the investor faces uncertainty on the *timing* of cash flows. An increased level of prepayments by borrowers, for example, means more cash is being paid, and there is more cash "passed through." An investor in a particular class or tranch of a CMO is presented with a set coupon. Further, prepayment risk is not shared equally across all tranches. The structure of the CMO tranches allows the investor to have greater certainty on the timing of cash flows.

19. First, mortgage-backed bonds are generally being issued by firms which are *retaining* the mortgages on their balance sheets. The mortgages are not sold off. This leads nicely to the second distinction: the mortgages are serving as *collateral* for the mortgage-backed bonds, but the mortgage payments are directly paid out to the investors in the bonds. The linkage between the mortgage payments and

the mortgage-backed bonds is not so direct as it would be with a pass-through or a CMO.

20. Prepayments on mortgages are sensitive to market interest rates. When interest rates fall, there are more prepayments, as borrowers are eager to take advantage of the better rates. Prepayments mean that principal is paid off earlier than the originally-scheduled amortization calls for. So, when prepayment occurs, the **PO** investor receives cash earlier. For **IO** investors, however, the prepayments mean there will be less interest received. Upon prepayment, there will be less principal left in the mortgage pool—and applying the contractual interest rate to a smaller principal amount means less interest (and less happy IO investors). Bottom line: IO and PO values respond differently to interest rate movements, because they respond differently to prepayment experience. See the text's Figure 7-10.

Problems:

1. Use the "present value of an annuity" formula. We know everything in the formula *except for* the payment or PMT. In general: $PV = PMT (PVIFA_{i/12, \, nx12})$. In the case at hand: $\$110,000 = PMT (PVIFA_{9\%/12, \, 15x12})$. If you're still looking up numbers in tables, you should find an annuity factor of something like 98.5934. Solving, we get PMT = $1,115.69.

   Alternatively, with a financial calculator or spreadsheet program, you can solve without looking up the annuity factor.

2. For the <u>first</u> payment:
   a) .09/12 is the interest rate *per month*. Multiply this by the beginning balance, or $110,000, to get interest of $825.
   b) The portion of PMT *not* devoted to interest will be the principal—or $1,115.69 less $825 = $290.69
   c) Balance = $110,000 less $290.69, or $109,709.31.

   For the <u>second</u> payment:
   a) .09/12 times $109,709.31 gives interest of $822.82. (Note that we're applying the interest rate to the now-smaller balance.)
   b) $1,115.69 - $822.82 = $292.87
   c) Balance = $109,709.31 - $292.87 = $109,416.44

3. With a 30-year amortization:
   a) $110,000 = PMT (PVIFA$_{.09/12,30x12}$). The annuity factor would be about 124.2819, and the resulting PMT = $885.08.
   b) Total payments (principal and interest), over the entire loan, come to $885.08 X 360 = $318,628.80. Since the original balance was $110,000, the difference—or $208,628.80—is the total amount of interest.
   c) Total payments, with 15-year amortization: $1,115.69 X 180 = $200,824.20. Given the $110,000 original balance, total interest is $90,824.20.

4. The general set-up for the payments is the same as in problem 1:
   a) $170,000 = PMT (PVIFA$_{6\%/12,\ 30x12}$). If you are working with a financial calculator: 360 payments, 6% annual (or 0.5% per month), $170,000 present value. Solve for PMT = $1,019.24 per month.
   b) Use the same loan amount (even though, with points, less ends up in the hands of the borrower, on net). We have: $170,000 = PMT (PVIFA$_{5.75\%\%/12,\ 30X12}$), and PMT = $992.07.
   c) Find the present value of the *difference* between the two monthly payments. That difference is $27.17 per month. The PV, over 360 payments, discounted at 5.75%/12, is $4,655.80. Now, compare this with what Bernard paid in up-front points: 1.5% X $170,000 = $2,550. (At the very beginning of the deal, Bernard actually received, on net, $170,000 - $2,550 = $167,450.) It looks like the *value* of the points ($4,655.80) is greater than what Bernard has to pay for them ($2,550).

   One additional comment is in order, however. The present value just computed assumes that Bernard will be paying this loan for the full 360 months. But it is quite possible that he will not have the loan for this length of time. If Bernard anticipates that his actual time in the loan is shorter than its stated maturity, it's possible that paying the points—in return for the lower monthly payments—would *not* be worthwhile.

5. First, figure out Tina's monthly payment.
   a) $90,000 = PMT (PVIFA$_{8\%/12,\ 30x12}$). PMT = $660.39.
   b) Tina will make a "balloon" payment at the end of five years—of an amount sufficient to pay off remaining principal. A financial calculator can tell you the amount owing at the end of the 60 monthly payments. Or, you can easily solve for it by getting the present value of a series of 300 payments of $660.39. My financial calculator gives me $85,562.87 for the balance due. (When I took the PV of 300 payments, I got a *slightly* larger figure—probably because I entered the payment to the nearest penny—whereas I had left fractions of cents in my calculator when using the first method.)
   Oh, just one more thing: the $85,562.87 is simply the amount of principal *after* the 60th payment—but don't forget that Tina would also be making the 60th payment at the same time. In other words, at the end of five years, she would be paying a total of $660.39 + $85,562.87 = $86,223.26.

   c) For the total interest, first total up all the payments to be made by Tina. Then deduct the initial amount of the loan, or $90,000.
   i) Totaling the first 60 installments: 60 X $660.30 = $39,623.40
   ii) Principal payment at end of five years: $85,562.87
   iii) Total payments overall = $125,186.27. So, the amount in excess of the $90,000 loan amount is the interest—$35,186.27.

CHAPTER 8
STOCK MARKETS

I.   SURVEYING THE TERRITORY: AN AERIAL VIEW

We find ourselves in the midst of equity securities now. What's different, compared to the previous two chapters? Well, buyers of bonds and mortgage-backed securities are creditors. They've been *promised* something. But the stockholders are owners, pure and simple. Stockholders are *residual claimants*—which is a fancy way of saying they haven't been promised much of anything. While the "upside" of a stock investment can be *way up*, the "downside" may be *nothing* at all.

With large corporations, the ownership may be dispersed, far and wide. You can own part of a company, yet feel very much like an "outsider." Of course, that's the beauty of it, at least from the company perspective. Companies can gain access to huge amounts of funding, by offering claims of ownership to a widely dispersed crowd. Highly developed markets—with lots of information flow—enhances the ability of companies to do this. Investors are more willing to participate when they can gain access to better information… and when there is a smooth-running market system in place, improving their ability to buy and sell.

In the early-2000s, we're all aware that stock market investors—perhaps some in the reading audience, right here—took some pretty big licks. (*Ouch!* Sorry... I really didn't mean to open up wounds that may still be healing!)   But that might provide all the more motivation for what Chapter 8 has to offer.

The major topics:

The Stock Markets: Chapter Overview

Stock Market Securities

Primary and Secondary Stock Markets

Stock Market Participants

Other Issues Pertaining to Stock Markets

International Aspects of Stock Markets

Appendix: Event Study Tests
(access the appendix at www.mhhe.com/sc2e)

II. DIGGING IN THE DIRT: A SUBTERRANEAN VIEW

Key terms

common stock	NYSE
residual claim	AMEX
limited liability	NASDAQ
dual-class firms	trading post
cumulative voting	specialists
proxy	market order
preferred stock	limit order
nonparticipating preferred stock	program trading
cumulative preferred stock	on-line trading
participating preferred stock	Dow Jones Industrial Average
noncumulative preferrred stock	NYSE Composite
primary markets	Standard & Poor's 500 Index
net proceeds	price-weighted
gross proceeds	value-weighted
underwriter's spread	market efficiency
syndicate	weak form
originating house	semistrong form
preemptive rights	strong form
red herring	random walk hypothesis
shelf registration	Regulation FD
secondary stock markets	ADR

Got a question?

1. The _____ refers to the price at which an investment bank sells a new issue to investors. But this is *not* the amount ultimately received by the issuer.

2. _____ was adopted by the SEC in October 2000, to combat selective disclosure of information by stock issuers.

3. This type of stock has an established, stated dividend payment, but the actual dividend in a given year *could* be even greater.
    This is: _____.

4. This is a voting arrangement in which all of a firm's directors are voted on simultaneously. The total votes per shareholder equals the number of shares held, multiplied by the number of directors to be elected. A shareholder could "lump together" all her votes and cast them for just one director, if desired.
    This is: _____.

5. Since common stock has the "lowest priority" for any cash distributions from corporation, we call it a: _____.

6. If stock market prices react quickly and appropriately to new, publicly-available information—but not to privately-held information—we would term the market to be _____ efficient.

7. The _____ are the markets in which funds are being raised, through *new* issues of securities.

8. The Standard & Poor's 500 Index is constructed by using a _____ methodology.

9. This is a type of stock market order, in which the investor expresses a willingness to trade, but at a specified price.
   This is a: _____.

10. If a common stock's price reacts very quickly and correctly to a new piece of information in the market, we would say that the market has a high degree of:
   _____.

11. Suppose a company is issuing new shares, and the shares must be offered first to existing shareholders—and in such a way that they can maintain their same ownership percentages. We say that the existing shareholders have:
   _____.

12. As a stockholder, you are *not liable* for the debts of the corporation. Your maximum loss is the amount you paid for the stock. This feature of stock is called: _____.

13. Prior to a security's registration, a preliminary version of the prospectus is distributed. This document is called the: _____.

14. This is a type of preferred stock requiring that any *missed* preferred dividends must be paid out *before* common stockholders receive any cash dividends.

15. _____ provides a venue for the trading of stocks not "listed" on a stock exchange. It is sometimes called an "over the counter" market, although it is actually comprised of many dealers, at various locations, linked electronically.

16. The Dow Jones Industrial Average is constructed by using a _____ methodology.

17. Sometimes investment banks form a "syndicate." What is such an arrangement? Why do the participants form it?

18. What might influence the size of the "underwriter's spread"?

19. What difference might "cumulative voting" make in electing corporate board members—in comparison to "straight voting"?

20. Distinguish "weak form" market efficiency from "semi-strong form" market efficiency.

Got a problem?

1. Jerry is looking at two possible stock investments. The *Established Corp.* is currently priced at $65 per share. It has been paying a $4 annual dividend, which Jerry expects will continue, at least for the next year. The *New Growth Corp.* is also currently priced at $65. It pays no dividend, and Jerry expects no change in the firm's dividend policy. Jerry just read the analysis of his favorite stock analyst, who is projecting next-year prices of: $71 for Established Corp. and $75 for New Growth Corp. Jerry faces a 31 percent tax rate on ordinary income, and a 20 percent tax rate on capital gains income.
    a) What are the pre-tax rates of return Jerry is expecting on *Established* and *New Growth*—assuming he trusts his favorite stock analyst?
    b) What are the after-tax rates of return Jerry is expecting?

2. Outer Limits Corp. has preferred stock outstanding. It par value is $20 per share. Its market price is currently $28 per share. The stock pays has a promised 4% annual dividend, and the dividend payment date is upon us.
    a) What dividend amount will the preferred stockholders expect, per share?
    b) Suppose that the actual dividends to be paid this year are $1.10 per share. What does this suggest about the *type* of preferred stock?

3. Consider a firm that is having an election for directors, with a **cumulative** voting scheme:

    Shares of common stock outstanding: 9,000,000 shares
    Directors up for election: 4
    Number of candidates: 5

    What is the *minimum* number of votes that will ensure a candidate's election to the board?

4. Northwoods Corp. has 10 million common shares outstanding. The stock price is $80. Northwoods will be issuing an additional 10 million shares, using a rights offering. Existing stockholders will receive one right per share, each one allowing a purchase of an additional share at a 5 percent discount from the going stock price—or $76 per share.
   a) What is the total value of the firm's stock *before* the issue of new shares?
   b) What will the total value of the firm's stock be *after* the new shares are issued?
   c) What will the price of a share be *after* the new issue?
   d) Some pre-issue shareholders may decide to sell their rights instead of exercising them. What will be the *value* of one right?

Web cruising ideas

1. Try to find the most recent *price* for a seat at the New York Stock Exchange. First head to the NYSE's web site. The address:

   http://www.nyse.com/home.html

   Also, look for historical seat prices, and try to find the highest price recorded there. (A little clue: there are lots of commas and zeros in these numbers. There's an old expression: "Sometimes, ya gotta pay to play.")

2. Sticking with that same NYSE site, try to find the *listing standards*—i.e., the requirements that must be met for a company to have its shares listed on the NYSE.

3. Let's not forget that important institution for smaller companies, NASDAQ. (And yes, it's important for some pretty big ones, too, like Microsoft.)

   http://www.nasdaq.com/

   One interesting area provides information on *extended* trading. Also, you might want to distinguish between *national market* issues and the *small caps*.

III.   WASHING UP... AND THE "ABC" AWARDS

A. The EASIEST THING in the chapter

Frankly, it's the *language* of the equity markets. With so many folks participating in equity markets—and yes, if you're still *day trading* and haven't lost your shirt, pull your hands away from the terminal and *wave*—a lot of the equity market lingo has become commonplace. Even school children have heard of Nasdaq, for goodness sake. I discovered how far things had come when a six-year old started asking me about the Dow Jones Industrial Average one day (*seriously,* I didn't make that up). Let us know if this book has become part of your neighborhood's first grade curriculum.

B. The HARDEST THING in the chapter

I suspect it's hard to appreciate the "goings-on" at a New York Stock Exchange trading post, using a textbook description and diagrams. Sometimes, you just have to *be there*.

C. The FUNNIEST THING in the chapter... or not

Words can be funny. This is especially true with the technical jargon in any field of study. So, what's funny here? Well...I can understand *weak form*. And I can understand *strong form*. Words like "strong" and "weak" are not a problem. But can you say *semi-strong form*—let's say at a social function—and keep a straight face? No, I'm not blaming our text's authors. The term has been with us for decades now. And no, I'm not bothered by the *concept*. It's the *words* that get me. Why not "semi-weak"? Or, maybe just "pretty darned strong"?

Thinking of *words* and *stock markets* brings to mind a person who's pretty darned good with *both*. Ever encountered television's Louis Rukeyser? He hosts *Louis Rukeyser's Wall Street*. (Hmm.... wonder where he came up with *that* catchy title?) Lou has quite a knack for talking about markets with words that *most* of us can understand. Be forewarned, however: Lou's been known to use a pun or two in his monologues—sometimes puns that can make even market-hardened investors groan. (I'm just glad I'm not the *only* one who looks for shreds of humor in financial markets.)

IV. CHECKING THE ANSWERS...FOR SECTION II

Terms:

1. gross proceeds
2. Regulation FD
3. participating preferred stock
4. cumulative voting
5. residual claim
6. semistrong form
7. primary markets
8. value-weighted
9. limit order
10. market efficiency
11. preemptive rights
12. limited liability
13. red herring
14. cumulative preferred stock
15. NASDAQ
16. price-weighted

Essays:

17. A syndicate is a group of investment banks that agree to underwrite an issuer's securities. Various members are "in" for various amounts of the total underwriting commitment. You might say it's a short-term partnership—formed for a particular deal. The investment bankers come together to spread the risk of a deal. In other words, even though one bank takes a "lead" role, it recognizes that underwriting the entire issue could be extremely risky. There may also be marketing and distribution advantages.

18. The key thing is *risk*. If there is greater uncertainty about the marketability of a new issue, the spread will be higher. In fact, if the risk is perceived to be prohibitively high, the issue will be peddled on a best efforts basis.

19. With a cumulative voting procedure, each shareholder has an aggregate number of votes equal to: shares owned X directors to be elected. But, in addition, the shareholders don't have to vote for each "seat" separately. Instead, they can lump together their votes—in the limit, a shareholder could cast *all* her votes for *one* director. In contrast, with straight voting, the shareholders will vote for each seat on the board separately. What all this means is that it is easier for minority shareholders to elect a seat on the board if there is cumulative voting. With straight voting, an investor with a majority of shares will dictate the outcome of the election.

20. The degree of market efficiency hinges on the quickness of investor response to new information. And the different versions of market efficiency relate to

different sets of information. We say that the market is "weakly" efficient if investors respond quickly to any information contained in the past prices in that market. So, if the price jumped up, say, four days ago, any information contained in that jump would have been used by market participants *at that time*. Four days after the price jump, the news is of no use to us, in determining a "good buy" in the market. (Likewise, knowing of a price jump from yesterday—or from four months ago—would do us no good.) The *most recent price* contains all the information we can get from the price series.

Why the term "weak"? Well, we're focusing on a narrow information set. If, in contrast, we say the market is "semi-strong" efficient—then we're saying that investors react quickly to new *publicly available* information. We're dealing with a much broader information set. It would contain news reports, company-released data, and on and on and on. If market prices *do* respond quickly to new information in this set, the market is even *more efficient*—hence, the term "semi-strong" efficiency.

Note that if a market is deemed to be "weakly" efficient, this does not preclude it from being even more strongly efficient. This is because the past prices *are part* of publicly available information.

Problems:

1. This question is simply reminding us of the importance of our neighborhood tax collector.
    a) For the pre-tax returns:

    $$\text{Established Corp.:} \quad \frac{\$71-\$65}{\$65} + \frac{\$4}{\$65} = \frac{\$10}{\$65} = 15.38\%$$

    $$\text{New Growth:} \quad \frac{\$75-\$65}{\$65} + \frac{\$0}{\$65} = \frac{\$10}{\$65} = 15.38\%$$

    b) For the after-tax returns:

    $$\text{Established Corp.:} \quad \frac{(\$71-\$65)(1-.20)}{\$65} + \frac{\$4(1-.31)}{\$65} = \frac{\$7.56}{\$65} = 11.63\%$$

    $$\text{New Growth:} \quad \frac{(\$75-\$65)(1-.20)}{\$65} + \frac{\$0(1-.31)}{\$65} = \frac{\$8}{\$65} = 12.31\%$$

2. The promised percentage is applied to the par value of the stock, so:
    a) $.04 \times \$20 = \$.80$
    b) If the actual dividend exceeds $.80 per share, then this preferred stock must be *participating* preferred stock.

3. The cumulative total number of votes (held by all the stockholders) is 36 million—or, on shares, multiplied by 4 seats to be elected.

   Since there are five candidates running, one-fifth, or 7,200,000 votes is "cut-off" number to ensure election. Well, strictly speaking, this number *plus one* vote would be needed—to avoid the possibility of a five-way tie, with 7,200,000 votes for each.

   A larger point: with the cumulative voting procedure, minority shareholders might be able to "lump together" their votes and get a candidate on the board.

4. Mostly, this problem is a matter of summing up value and keeping track of shares.
   a) Total value, before new issue: 10 million shares X $80 = $800 million
   b) Total value, after new issue: "old value" + "new value"
      Or, $800 million + (10 million X $76 per share) = $1,560 million
   c) Price per share, after new issue:
      Total shareholder value/total number of shares
      = $1,560 million/20 million shares
      = $78 per share
   d) The pre-issue shareholders can purchase new shares at a price of $76 + one right. But a share will be *worth* $78. So, the value of one right is $2.

CHAPTER 9
FOREIGN EXCHANGE MARKETS

I.   SURVEYING THE TERRITORY: AN AERIAL VIEW

Now, just how many times have you heard term "global economy"? Roughly speaking, and speaking only for myself, I'd say about 937 times—and that's just over the last month or so! In a sense, this isn't anything new. The world has always been a *globe*, for goodness sake. So, what else could the economy be… cubical?

Okay, okay… but you know the *real* point here. Trading across international borders is commonplace; it's an expected facet of business today. And so, we need to be conversant with the language of international finance. A lot of the discussion has to do with an apparent "bookkeeping" complication—in particular, we've got to convert U.S. dollars to Japanese yen, or British pounds, or whatever. And what makes it all a bit *more* than an ordinary bookkeeping problem is that the *ratio or exchange rate* for the conversion is not fixed. Instead of just worrying about the price of goods in Japan, or the price of credit in Japan, we also have to worry about how *our own domestic* currency will convert into yen. And, instead of worrying ourselves to death, it may be worthwhile to *relieve* ourselves from the worry, through *hedging* activities.

It sounds complicated. And yes, it *can* be complicated… but it turns out that the behavior of market participants serves to link things together. In fact, this is where *purchasing power parity* and *interest rate parity* come into play. At the risk of over-simplifying, international players are looking around for relative prices that make some deals seem a little *too* good. As they take advantage of them, prices change. What sorts of prices? Well…spot exchange rates... forward exchange rates... and interest rates offered in different countries.

Chapter topics:

Foreign Exchange Markets and Risk: Chapter Overview

Background and History of Foreign Exchange Markets

Foreign Exchange Rates and Transactions

Interaction of Interest Rates, Inflation, and Exchange Rates

Balance of Payment Accounts

II. DIGGING IN THE DIRT: A SUBTERRANEAN VIEW

Key terms

    foreign exchange markets
    foreign exchange rate
    foreign exchange risk
    currency depreciation
    currency appreciation
    spot foreign exchange transaction
    forward foreign exchange transaction
    net exposure
    net long in a currency
    net short in a currency
    open position
    purchasing power parity (PPP)
    interest rate parity theorem (IRPT)
    balance of payment accounts
    current account
    capital accounts

Got a question?

1. A _____ is one where an exchange of currencies is agreed upon, at a specified exchange rate, but with the exchange to occur at some future point in time.

2. The _____ is the price at which one nation's currency can be exchanged for another.

3. If a financial institution buys British pounds in a speculative trade, without hedging, we describe its position as an: _____.

4. The _____ states that the change in exchange rates between two countries' currencies is proportional to the difference in the inflation rates in the two countries.

5. Today, we notice that a given amount of Japanese yen can buy *more* U.S. dollars. We would say that the yen is demonstrating: _____.

6. Suppose that U.S. banks have *sold more* German marks than they have *purchased*. To describe the position of these institutions, we would say that the banks are

7. Transactions between citizens of one country with citizens of other countries is summarized in the: _____.

8. A financial institution's overall foreign exchange risk exposure in a given currency is called its: _____.

9. Suppose that BankAmerica buys Canadian dollars with U.S. dollars. The exchange of currencies takes place today, at today's exchange rate. This is a: _____.

10. If we observed a *negative balance* in the _____ portion of the U.S. balance of payments, it would indicate that U.S. investors purchased *more* foreign assets than foreign investors purchased U.S. assets.

11. This theory implies that an investor who hedges in the foreign exchange market will realize the same return—whether investing domestically or in a foreign country.
    This is: _____.

12. Briefly, what does the theory of **purchasing power parity** (PPP) suggest?

13. A U.S. banking institution takes in $300 million of 1-year deposits. It contemplates the following allocation of the funds: (a) make 1-year loans to domestic, U.S. borrowers in the amount $200 million, and (b) make 1-year loans to Japanese borrowers, in the dollar-equivalent amount of $100 million—but the Japanese loans would be made in yen.
    a) Explain the risk associated with such a transaction.
    b) Explain how the bank could *hedge* the risk.
    c) If the bank follows your advice in part (b), what is expected to happen in one year?
    d) What does the bank "give up" by hedging?

Got a problem?

1. A U.S. firm is buying a piece of Japanese equipment for 5 million yen. Payment is due now. We see two relevant, current exchange rates: (i) 125.60 yen per dollar, and (ii) 0.07962 dollars per yen. How many dollars will it take for the U.S. firm to meet its obligation?

2. If we know that the Hong Kong dollar is worth $ .1232 in U.S. dollars, how much is the U.S. dollar worth in *Hong Kong dollars*?

3. Refer to the preceding problem, and assume the same exchange rate between Hong Kong dollars and U.S. dollars. Now, suppose a U.S. importing concern wants to buy a shipment of Hong Kong produced ceramics. The price of the shipment, in Hong Kong dollars, is (HK)$ 5,800,000.
    a) How much is the price, in U.S. dollars?
    b) Now, suppose several weeks pass before the transaction is completed and payment is required. The Hong Kong price remains the same as before. But the Hong Kong dollar is now worth $.1290 in U.S. dollars. What has happened to the price of the shipment, in U.S. dollars?
    c) In cases like this, how could an importer have *hedged* against the foreign currency risk?

4. Suppose that British (UK) pounds are worth $1.5200 in U.S. dollars. Suppose prices of U.S. goods rises 4% and prices of UK goods rises by 6%. According to purchasing power parity (PPP), what will happen to the exchange rate between pounds and dollars?

5. Suppose that the *spot* exchange rate between U.S. dollars and the British pound is $1.4586 dollars per pound. The 3-month *forward* exchange rate is $1.4504 dollars per pound. If a risk-free, 3-month British bank deposit offers an interest rate of 2.20%, what should the 3-month rate be for a U.S. deposit?

6. Suppose that the *spot* exchange rate between U.S. dollars and Japanese yen is $.00797 dollars per yen. The 6-month *forward* exchange rate is $.008057 dollars per yen. If a risk-free, 6-month Japanese bank deposit offers an interest rate of 3.50%, what should the 6-month rate be for a U.S. deposit?

Web cruising ideas

1. There are lots of places to look up exchange rate information. One site with a nifty currency conversion feature is Bloomberg. Here's the address:

   http://www.bloomberg.com/markets/currency/currcalc.html

2. Chapter 9 brings up the European Union. Well, you can learn a lot more about it...you guessed it...at their web site:

   http://europa.eu.int/index_en.htm#

3. There's a European Central Bank, too:

   http://www.ecb.int/

III. WASHING UP... AND THE "ABC" AWARDS

A. The EASIEST THING in the chapter

The easiest thing for me is the text's **Figure 9-1**, which shows the difference between a spot transaction and a forward transaction. It's such a simple picture that it may be totally unappreciated. But a picture like this is worth a thousand words of definition.

B. The HARDEST THING in the chapter

Example 9-2, Calculating the Return of Foreign Exchange Transactions, is one that takes some time and concentration—but does have a high payoff. (Likewise, for **Examples 9-3** and **9-4**, which build on **9-2**) The idea there is to demonstrate—with the numbers—how transactions involving more than one currency bring about exchange rate risk. By the way, you might note that some special assumptions are being made, to allow us to focus on just the exchange rate risk. With "matched duration," we don't worry about interest rate risk. Also, credit risk is assumed away. (How I wish we could *assume away* such things in real life!)

C. The FUNNIEST THING in the chapter... or not

The idea lurking behind purchasing power parity is that the *same* basket of goods should cost the *same* as we go from country to country. Well, the folks at a well-known business periodical, *The Economist*, have a way of bringing PPP down to an understandable, albeit greasy level. They track the price across countries of a *very particular* basket. What's in the basket? One thing: a McDonalds' Big Mac. According to *The Economist*, the famous sandwich is sold in something like 120 countries! Observed pricing discrepancies are taken as evidence of an *under-* or *over-valued* currency. Check it out sometime, at:

http://www.economist.com/markets/bigmac/about.cfm

IV. CHECKING THE ANSWERS...FOR SECTION II

Terms:
1. forward foreign exchange transaction
2. foreign exchange rate
3. open position
4. purchasing power parity theorem (PPP)
5. currency appreciation
6. net short in a currency
7. balance of payment accounts
8. net exposure
9. spot foreign exchange transaction
10. capital accounts
11. interest rate parity theorem

Essays:
12. PPP implies that foreign currency exchange rates will adjust to reflect differences in inflation rates on the international sphere. If prices in the USA are rising faster than prices in Germany, consumers will be more inclined to purchase Germany's goods. There will be a larger demand for German marks, relative to the demand for U.S. dollars. The value of the mark (in U.S. dollar terms) will rise. People, in other words, will flock towards the "best deals." And their flocking will change exchange rates.

13. Banking essay:
    a) First, there is likely to be default risk on the loans—but the question does not address this aspect of the deal. More obvious here is the foreign exchange risk inherent in the bank's plan. By making the loan in yen, the bank will be receiving its payoff in yen. There is risk in terms of how the yen/dollar exchange rate will change over time.
    b) The bank can hedge the risk by engaging in a forward foreign exchange transaction at the time the Japanese loan is made. In particular, the bank would want to *sell* Japanese yen in the forward foreign exchange market. How much? Sell an amount equal to the amount of the loan, plus the interest proceeds on the loan. The question does not specify an interest rate, so we can only say the amount would be at least $100 million. The desired maturity (or "delivery date") of the forward exchange contract would be coincident with the maturity of the loan.
    c) When we reach maturity of the loan, the bank will be receiving yen as repayment on the Japanese loan. At the same time, however, the bank will be delivering yen on its forward market contract. If the bank did its homework correctly, the amount it receives on the loan payoff will be the same as (or at least close to) the amount it is delivering on the forward contract. It has locked in an exchange rate by using the forward market. It knows in advance how many dollars it will be receiving for the yen it delivers.

d) By engaging in the forward market transaction, the bank is giving up the opportunity for a *possible profit from changing exchange rates*. For example, if the bank had *not* hedged, and over time the Japanese yen "strengthened" against the dollar, then the bank would have profited from the appreciating yen. The yen received in the loan payoff would be worth *more* dollars. The bank gives up this opportunity when it decides to hedge.

Problems:

1. We could use either one of the given exchange rates, because each is simply a *reciprocal* of the other. But using the second one (dollars/yen) is perhaps a bit more direct:

$$\frac{dollars}{yen} \times yen = dollars$$

$$\$.007962 \times 5,000,000 = \$39,810 \text{ owed to the Japanese supplier}$$

2. If a Hong Kong dollar is worth U.S. $ .1232, then a U.S. dollar is worth (1/.1232) or 8.1169 Hong Kong dollars.

3. Start with the exchange rate in the preceding problem.
   a) HK$ 5,800,000 X .1232 = US $ 714,560
   b) Now, applying the new exchange rate, the U.S. dollar price has gone up to $748,200—a difference of $33,640.
   c) When the transaction was initiated, the importer would want to eliminate the uncertainty created by the unknown exchange rate. The importer could *buy* Hong Kong dollars in a *forward market* transaction. This would lock in an exchange rate, and thereby "hedge" the risk.

4. According to PPP:

   Inflation rate, US – Inflation rate, GB = $\dfrac{\text{Change in spot exchange rate, US\$/UK}}{\text{Initial spot rate, US\$/UK}}$

   $.04 - .06 = \dfrac{\text{Change in spot exchange rate, US\$/UK}}{\text{Initial spot rate, US\$/UK}} = -.02$

   In other words, the exchange rate (of dollars per pound) would *fall by 2%.* The new exchange rate would be (1-.02)($1.5200) = $1.4896.

5. Use the interest rate parity relationship to solve for the U.S. interest rate.

$$1 + i_{USt} = \left(\frac{1}{S_t}\right) \times \left(1 + i_{UK,t}\right) \times F_t$$

where S = \$/pound—spot exchange rate, and F = \$/pound—forward exchange rate.

$$1 + i_{USt} = \left(\frac{1}{1.4586}\right) \times (1 + .022) \times 1.4504 = 1.0163$$

So, the U.S. interest rate should be .0163 or 1.63%

6. Use the interest rate parity relationship to solve for the U.S. interest rate.

$$1 + i_{USt} = \left(\frac{1}{S_t}\right) \times \left(1 + i_{Jap}\right) \times F_t$$

where S = \$/yen—spot exchange rate, and F = \$/yen—forward exchange rate.

$$1 + i_{USt} = \left(\frac{1}{.00797}\right) \times (1 + .035) \times .008057 = 1.0463$$

So, the U.S. interest rate should be .0463 or 4.63%

CHAPTER 10
DERIVATIVE SECURITIES MARKETS

I. SURVEYING THE TERRITORY: AN AERIAL VIEW

Note that word at the top: *derivative.* Values of contracts described in this chapter are *derived from* other things. Also, note another word in the preceding sentence: *contracts.* Folks are entering into contractual agreements. The agreement might, for example, give someone the *right* to do something in the future—maybe the right to buy Microsoft stock at a certain price. In this case the value of that *right* is linked, or *derived from* the value of Microsoft stock. In a different agreement, someone might be *obligated* to do something in the future—like the obligation to sell 5,000 bushels of grain at a certain price. Here, the value of the obligation depends on the value of the grain. (By the way, that *right to buy* Microsoft is a *call option.* And what about the *obligation* to sell grain? Now we're dealing with a *futures or forward contract.*)

Yeah, this is still pretty darned ambiguous. You've got to dig into some details to appreciate it.

Chapter topics:

Derivative Securities: Chapter Overview

Forwards and Futures

Options

Regulation of Futures and Options Markets

Swaps

Caps, Floors, and Collars

International Aspects of Derivatives Security Markets

**Appendix: Black-Scholes Option Pricing Model
(accessible at www.mhhe.com/sc2e)**

II. DIGGING IN THE DIRT: A SUBTERRANEAN VIEW

Key terms

derivative security
spot contract
forward contract
futures contract
marked to market
initial margin
maintenance margin
CBT
CME
open-outcry
floor broker
professional traders
position traders
day traders
scalpers
long position
short position
clearinghouse
open interest
option
American option
European option
call option
put option

exercise price
option premium
in the money
out of the money
at the money
writing a call
writing a put
intrinsic value of an option
time value of an option
CBOE
stock index option
call on a futures contract
put on a futures contract
swap
interest rate swap
swap buyer
notional principal
swap seller
swap markets
currency swap
cap
floor
collar

Hey, the length of the list above may have just set a chapter *record*!

Got a question?

1. Some folks will buy (or sell) a futures contract for a *very* short period of time. They are looking for a profit—rather than trying to "protect" something else they own—and the "short period of time" could be just a matter of minutes. These traders are called: _____.

2. This person is a member of the futures exchange, and is one who places trades from the public.
    This is a: _____.

3. A _____ is an agreement for the immediate exchange of an asset for funds. The funds and the asset will "flow" at (or close to) the time of the agreement.

4. With a _____ contract, one party acquires the right to buy a specified security from another party, at a specified price, and for a specified period of time.

5. This is a particular kind of option—it could be a put or a call—which can be exercised at any time up to a specified expiration time.
This is the: _____.

6. Two parties have agreed to exchange interest payments. A "floating rate payment" is exchanged for a "fixed rate payment."
This is the: _____.

7. A _____ is basically a call option on interest rates. As interest rates rise above a specified level, the owner receives payment.

8. The _____ is a deposit that buyers and sellers of futures contracts must make at the inception of a futures contract, to ensure that terms of the contract will be met.

9. A _____ is a financial security whose payoff is linked to another, previously issued security. There are several types of such securities—each having a somewhat different way of establishing payoffs.

10. Prices on outstanding futures contracts are _____, meaning that the futures prices are adjusted each day, reflecting current market conditions.

11. The _____ is an exchange, which offers trading on Treasury notes, Treasury bonds, Federal funds, and Eurodollars, among others.

12. Jamie wants to sell the right to sell 100 shares of Cisco Systems stock. We can also say that Jamie is interested in _____ on Cisco.

13. The buyer of a _____ has purchased the right to buy a specified, underlying futures contract.

14. In contrast to futures and options markets, _____ are governed by very little regulation, although a global trade association exists, which sets codes and standards.

15. A call option on General Motors' stock exists, having an exercise price of $40 and expiration in March. Today, GM stock is selling at $40 per share. We would describe the call option as being _____.

16. Explain how to determine the *intrinsic value* of a *call option* on a stock.

17. Explain:
    a) the nature of a collar, and
    b) the motivation for taking such a position.

18. When comparing futures and forward contracts:
    a) What is similar?
    b) What is different?

19. A *call option* on Intel stock has an exercise price of $135. It is selling for a premium of $12. Intel's stock price is currently $145.
    a) If you buy "one contract," how much will you be paying?
    b) Is the call option "in the money," or not? Explain.
    c) If you *sell* one contract, what would you be hoping for, to make your option sale a profitable one?

Got a problem?

1. The Chicago Board of Trade offers futures contracts on the Dow-Jones Industrial Average. One particular contract has a dollar multiplier of $10—meaning, to determine the size of your obligation on one contract, multiply the DJ Average by $10. Now, suppose you *buy* three contracts, when the futures price is 8450. Later, at the delivery date for your contract, the DJ Industrial Average is at 8537. Did you *gain* or *lose* on this contract? How much?

2. There is a mini-Dow contract (on the DJ Industrial Average, and available at the Chicago Board of Trade), which has a multiplier of $5. The size of one contract is $5 times the Dow Jones Industrial Average. Your friend Tom holds a diversified portfolio of stocks that's currently worth $43,000. Tom has some concerns about the stock market over the next three months, but he doesn't want to sell the stocks right now. Today's futures price for the DJ Industrials, for delivery in three months, is 8600.
    a) How could Tom use the mini-Dow contract to hedge his stock portfolio?
    b) Suppose Tom "puts on the hedge." Later, at the delivery date of the futures contract, we see that: (i) the Dow Jones Industrials are at 8400, and (ii) Tom's stock portfolio value is $40,850. What has happened to Tom's overall situation—from his stock *and* the futures contract?
    c) What if stocks had *risen* instead? Would Tom have been "un-hedged"?

3. Consider a *call option* on Intel stock, having an exercise price of $135. It is selling for a *premium* of $12. And Intel's stock price is currently $145. (Same option as in an earlier, essay question.)
   a) What is the "intrinsic value" of the call option?
   b) Suppose you *buy* the call option today and hold it until expiration. What is your *profit* or *loss*, given the following possible prices for Intel stock: $120, $135, and $150.
   c) Suppose you *sold* the call option today. Assuming no exercise occurs until the expiration day, what is your profit or loss—given the same possible prices listed in part (b)?

4. Sticking with the current Intel stock price of $145 (preceding question), suppose there is a *put option*, with an exercise price of $135, and having a *premium* of $1. Now answer parts (a), (b), and (c) of the preceding question—but as applied to the *put option*.

5. A call option exists, written on IBM stock, and having an exercise price of $70. IBM's stock price today is $79. The call option's premium today is $11.50.
   a) What is the call's *intrinsic value*?
   b) What is the call's *time value*

Web cruising ideas

1. Go to the web site for the Chicago Board of Trade. Here's the address:

   http://www.cbot.com/

   Try this: see if you can track down the "chronological history" of the CBOT. Just when did this institution emerge from the Midwestern wilderness?

   If you want to dig into some specifics, take a look at information on the "Dow Complex," i.e., futures contracts related to the Dow Jones Industrial Average.

   http://www.cbot.com/cbot/dow/page/0,2611,1,00.html

2. Let's not forget options. Take a look at the Chicago Board Options Exchange site, and maybe especially, the product descriptions page:

   http://www.cboe.com/OptProd/understanding_products.asp

III.　WASHING UP... AND THE "ABC" AWARDS

A.　The EASIEST THING in the chapter

This is a tough call—because the *easiest thing* is finding *hard stuff* in Chapter 10! But I'll say it's the *spot market* discussion. Why? Because the spot market is just about all the financial market stuff *before* we came across derivatives! In other words, you have already learned about spot market activities ... but nobody bothered to call them "spot market activities." The stock market, the bond market... when talking about these markets, we were always talking about transactions for delivery "on the spot." It was simply *understood* before. But now, we need a term to distinguish those kinds of transactions from various others.

B.　The HARDEST THING in the chapter

Hmm... so many candidates, and *so little time*! This may be cheating, but I'll pick something not fully covered in the text: the Black-Scholes option-pricing model. The text provides some introductory, get-acquainted *advertising* for the model. And while it's a model built on intuitively comfortable economic logic, the actual formula scares the wits out of many good and noble souls. (So be thankful you're getting off a bit easy by not being bombarded with the details.) But be forewarned: if you continue in finance, the Black-Scholes model will surface again...and again... and again. It's *that important*.

C.　The FUNNIEST THING in the chapter... or not

Well, once again, I'm not exactly rolling in the aisle with laughter. But, what the heck, let's make our own fun. First, go to the Chicago Board of Trade's web site. Browse around to find CBOT's on-line store. Now, step right up and order an incredibly funny-looking *action trader* necktie.

Hmm... a *necktie*... for *fun*? You're right—we gotta do better than that. So how about a *bulls and bears reversible puppet*? No, I'm not making this up. I saw it right there at CBOT's web site. (Better act now—I'm sure supplies must be dwindling fast!)

Oh yeah... now what to do when it arrives...you know, for *fun*? Well...make up the world's first puppet show based on the CBOT, of course.

IV. CHECKING THE ANSWERS...FOR SECTION II

Terms:
1. scalpers
2. floor broker
3. spot market
4. call option
5. American option
6. interest rate swap
7. cap
8. initial margin
9. derivative
10. marked to market
11. CBT (for Chicago Board of Trade)
12. writing a put
13. call on a futures contract
14. swap markets
15. at the money

Essays:
16. The intrinsic value if the call option is the *maximum* of: (a) the current stock price minus the option's exercise price, or (b) zero. If the current stock price is *greater than or equal* to the exercise price, you could view the intrinsic value as: the holder's payoff if the call option were exercised *right now*. And, what if the current stock price is *less* than the exercise price? Well, the holder of the option is *not obligated* to exercise, so the call cannot have a payoff less than zero.

17. The party who buys a *collar* is buying a *cap* and selling a *floor* at the same time. Such a party wants protection from rising market interest rates—that's where the "cap part" fits in. But what about the "floor part"? Well, selling the floor generates a premium, which can help to offset the cost of buying the cap. Of course, selling the floor brings with it an obligation too. If rates should *fall* below the floor rate, our collar owner will have to pay. The collar-buyer has put himself in a position to "win" from rate increases and to "lose" from rate decreases.

18. Futures contracts *and* forward contracts are *both* contracts for "deferred delivery." With both, a seller and buyer *promise* to exchange an asset for funds, and the asset delivery occurs in the future. But the forward contract can include specifications that are tailored by the buyer and sell. In contrast, a futures contract is an exchange-sponsored contract. There will be standardized contractual features with the futures contract. There will also be "marking to market" with the futures contract, which will affect how the funds flow over the life of the contract.

19. On the Intel call:
   a) The standard option contract is for 100 shares, even though the published option premium appears on a "per share" basis. So, you will be paying $12 times 100 shares, or $1,200 (ignoring brokerage commission).
   b) The call option is "in the money." The holder of the call has the right to buy Intel stock at a price of $135—which is *less* than the going price of Intel. So, if the holder wanted, he/she could exercise now and have a positive payoff (assuming it's an American option, of course).
   c) The *sellers* of the call (the call "writers") are hoping that *exercise does not occur*—so that the call premium can be pocketed, with no requirement to deliver the Intel stock. So, in essence, the sellers are hoping that the Intel stock price *falls below the call's exercise price*.

Problems:

1. At initiation of the deal, you promised to *buy* the index, for a "price" of 8450. (Actually the "8450" is an index number, linked to the prices of the 30 Dow Jones stocks.) You have agreed to pay $10 X 8450 X 3 contracts, or $253,500. At the delivery date—even though there's no actual delivery of stocks with this kind of contract—the DJ industrials have risen to 8537. So, you stand to "receive" something worth $10 X 8537 X 3 contracts, or $256,110. You've gained the difference, or $2,610.

2. Note that Tom holds a *diversified* portfolio, so we'll make the reasonable assumption that the Dow Jones Industrial Average (30 stocks) behaves at least *something* like his portfolio.
   a) One contract, at the current futures price, has a value of $5 X 8600, or $43,000. (You're right, this happens to be just the same as his stock portfolio value—which would only happen by *incredible accident* in the real world! But sometimes poetic license helps us make a larger point more clearly.) So, it would make sense for Tom to *sell* exactly *one* futures contract.
   b) At the delivery date: Tom has lost $2,150 in value of his stock portfolio. But he has *gained* on his futures contract. Remember that he promised to *sell* something, for $43,000. But at delivery, he is "receiving" something worth $5 X 8200, or $41,000. He pockets the difference, or $2,000. *Overall*, Tom has lost a net amount of $2,150 - $2,000, or $150. Tom achieved a hedge—he lost a lot less than he would have without the future position. But he was not *perfectly* hedged. Why? Because his portfolio of stocks was not *exactly* the same as those in the Dow Jones Industrials.
   c) Not really. If stock prices went up, perhaps Tom would have some "after the fact" regrets about bothering with the futures contract in the first place. But his results, at least qualitatively, are the same as before. He would gain on one thing (now, his stock portfolio). And he would lose on something else (the futures contract).

3. On the call option:
   a) The intrinsic value is the current stock price ($145) less the exercise price ($135), or $10. Note: this is on a "per share" basis.

   b) If you *bought* the call:
   <u>At Intel price of $120</u>:
   The option will not be exercised, and so no "payoff" will occur. But the call option holder had to pay $12 for the option. So, the holder experiences a loss of $12. Or, for one contract, the loss would be $12 times 100 shares, or $1,200. (But it is very common to simply identify the profit or loss on a "per share" basis.)
   <u>At Intel price of $135</u>:
   Again, there will be no exercise. There will be a loss of $12.
   <u>At Intel price of $150</u>:
   The option will be exercised; the holder received a payoff of $150 minus the exercise price of $135, or $15. But $12 was paid initially for the call. The net profit will be $3.

   c) If you *sold* the call:
   <u>At Intel price of $120</u>:
   No exercise occurs, so the seller simply "walks away" with the call premium. The seller profits, with the profit equal to the premium received: $12 (on a "per share" basis).
   <u>At Intel price of $135</u>:
   "Ditto" with the above. Profit is $12.
   <u>At Intel price of $150</u>:
   Exercise occurs, prompting a "payoff" from *seller* to *buyer* of $15. Given the initial $12 premium received, the *loss* is $3.

   General comment: The call owner *gains* what the call seller *loses*—and *vice versa*!

4. On the put option:
   a) Intrinsic value: Note that the put option's exercise price is *below* the going price of Intel—the put is "out of the money." But the put cannot have negative value. So, its intrinsic value is zero.

   b) If you *bought* the put:
   <u>At Intel price of $120</u>:
   The buyer exercises, receiving a payoff of $15. But the holder paid $1 for the put option. Net profit is $14.
   <u>At Intel price of $135</u>:
   There will be no exercise. There will be a loss of the premium, or $1.
   <u>At Intel price of $150</u>:
   No exercise; a net loss of the premium, or $1.

c) If you *sold* the put:
    <u>At Intel price of $120</u>:
    Seller "makes good" on the exercise, losing $15. But recognizing the $1 premium received initially, the net loss is $14.
    <u>At Intel price of $135</u>:
    No exercise occurs. Sell simply keeps the $1 premium—and that's the profit.
    <u>At Intel price of $150</u>:
    No exercise occurs. Again, the seller has a profit of $1.

5. For the IBM call option:
   a) *Intrinsic value:* Think about the consequences of an exercise today. You buy IBM of $70, when it's actually worth $79. You keep the difference, or $9. That's the intrinsic value. (Remember, the intrinsic value cannot go below zero.)
   b) The option is trading at a price of $11.50, or $2.50 above its intrinsic value. This is the *time value*.

CHAPTER 11
COMMERCIAL BANKS

I. SURVEYING THE TERRITORY: AN AERIAL VIEW

This chapter gives a broad view of commercial banking. A commercial bank is just one type of *depository* institution—which, by the way, includes savings associations, savings banks, and credit unions. Depositories are important enough to warrant quite a bit of attention in our text, starting with Chapter 11, and running through the next *three* chapters.

But, getting back to *commercial banking*—the label itself is really a bit misleading. Historically, commercial banks were the institutions of prime importance in making *commercial loans*—i.e., loans to businesses. But they certainly deal with consumers as well, both in their lending and deposit-taking activities. Furthermore, the casual observer will find it very hard to distinguish between commercial banks and their depository institution cousins, such as savings banks or credit unions. They all take in deposits. And they all make loans. The lines of demarcation are looking rather fuzzy these days.

The chapter topics:

Commercial Banks as a Sector of the Financial Institutions Industry: Chapter Overview

Definition of a Commercial Bank

Balance Sheets and Recent Trends

Size, Structure, and Composition of the Industry

Industry Performance

Technology in Commercial Banking

Regulators

Global Issues

II.   DIGGING IN THE DIRT: A SUBTERRANEAN VIEW

Key terms

transactions accounts	money center bank
NOW account	interest rate spread
negotiable CDs	net interest margin
equity capital	noncurrent loans
off-balance-sheet asset	net charge-offs
off-balance-sheet liability	net operating income
trust services	float
correspondent banking	lockbox services
megamerger	ATM
economies of scale	POS debit card
economies of scope	on-line banking
X efficiencies	smart card
diseconomies of scale	FDIC
economic rents	OCC
community bank	dual banking system
regional or superregional bank	Federal Reserve System
federal funds market	holding company

Got a question?

1. This is a larger-size bank, located in a major financial center, which participates in national and international money markets.
    This is the: _____.

2. Let's say a banking firm is able to lower its average costs by producing a wider variety of financial service products.
    This bank is demonstrating: _____.

3. This is the provider of federally sponsored deposit insurance for banks and savings institutions.
    This is the: _____.

4. This is a particular kind of deposit account. It has check-writing privileges, but also can pay interest.
    This is the: _____.

5. A bank may make a loan commitment to a customer—agreeing to lend at some future time, and with certain conditions. No asset entry appears on the bank's balance sheet at the time the commitment is made. But later on, the commitment may result in a loan, which does appear on the balance sheet.
    The commitment provides an example of an: _____.

6. _____ refers to a bank providing banking services to *other* banks—in particular, to other banks lacking the staff to perform the services themselves.

7. If a bank can lower its average cost of production by operating at a higher level—say, with larger asset size or larger deposit size—then the bank is demonstrating _____.

8. In the United States, there are two levels of chartering for commercial banks: a national bank charter or a state bank charter.
   This "two level" system is referred to as: _____.

9. When a bank borrows on a short-term basis from another bank, it is participating in the: _____.

10. Often a _____ owns one or more commercial banks. Such firms in the banking industry are regulated and examined by the Federal Reserve System.

11. The _____ is a part of the U.S. Treasury, and its primary function is to charter national banks.

12. This is a bank which specializes in retail-oriented, or consumer banking. It tends to be on the smaller end of the size spectrum.
    This is the: _____.

13. A bank's _____ consists mainly of common and preferred stock, surplus or additional paid-in capital, and retained earnings.

14. If, as a bank increases its scale or size of operations, its average cost of production rises, it is experiencing _____.

15. _____ refers to the time between the deposit of a check and the availability of the funds to the depositor.

16. The _____ allows the user to store and spend money, by using a card with a chip storage device.

17. The _____ allows the user to access their banks accounts around the clock. Customers can withdraw cash and pay bills from such devices.

18. The _____ is the bank's interest income less its interest expense, divided by the bank's earning assets.

19. Explain how the balance sheet of a *depository* institution differs from the balance sheet of a non-financial firm.

20. Bank assets generally differ from bank liabilities, in terms of maturity and liquidity. Explain these differences.

Got a problem?

Believe it or not, this chapter allows you to take a break from calculations. Put your calculator on the shelf... and let it cool off.

Web cruising ideas

There are a number of useful web sites maintained by the Federal government's bank regulators. Here are a couple of them:

1. The Federal Financial Institutions Examination Council (FFIEC), which contains useful links to various regulatory agencies:
     http://www.ffiec.gov/

2. Here's a particular "avenue," off the FFIEC site, for the *National Information Center*. It's maintained by the Federal Reserve System, and, among other things, provides information on the 50 *largest banks* and 50 *largest bank holding companies*.
     http://www.ffiec.gov/nic/default.HTM

III.   WASHING UP… AND THE "ABC" AWARDS

A. The EASIEST THING in the chapter

This one's easy: defining a ***depository institution***. I mean, really—isn't it a "self-defining" term?

B. The HARDEST THING in the chapter

In an overview chapter like this one, it's hard to gain much depth—and that is especially true when covering "off balance sheet activities." Take a look at Table 11-3, just to review some of the categories. There is a lot of stuff that qualifies as *off balance sheet* banking activity.

C. The FUNNIEST THING in the chapter… or not

What do bankers do for fun? (Well, okay… *beside*s counting all that money?) For some bankers, evidently, *fun* means *baseball*.

Ever hear of *Bank One Ballpark*? It's home to the Arizona Diamondbacks.
http://arizona.diamondbacks.mlb.com/NASApp/mlb/ari/ballpark/ari_ballpark_history.jsp

How about *Comerica Park*?
http://detroit.tigers.mlb.com/NASApp/mlb/det/ballpark/det_ballpark_history.jsp

And we don't want to forget *PNC Park*.
http://pittsburgh.pirates.mlb.com/NASApp/mlb/pit/ballpark/pit_ballpark_history.jsp

IV.   CHECKING THE ANSWERS...FOR SECTION II

Terms:
1. money center bank
2. economies of scope
3. FDIC
4. NOW account
5. off-balance-sheet asset
6. correspondent banking
7. economies of scale
8. the dual banking system
9. federal funds market
10. holding company
11. OCC (or Office of the Comptroller of the Currency)
12. community bank
13. equity capital
14. diseconomies of scale
15. float
16. smart card
17. ATM (for automated teller machine)
18. net interest margin

Essays:
19. A depository institution—like a commercial bank—has *deposits* as a major liability. The funds provided by depositors are invested or loaned out—and so, we observe *loans* and other *financial assets* on the asset side of the balance sheet. In contrast, non-financial firms are likely to hold bank deposits, and to borrow from banks. Hence, looking at their balance sheets, we will see *deposits* among the assets, and *loans* among the liabilities. Also, the non-financial firm's other assets are likely to be heavily weighted toward tangible, non-financial assets.

20. Banks assets, like loans, are generally of longer maturity than bank liabilities. To illustrate, note that bank liabilities consist primarily of deposits, and many of these have very short maturity—or, in the case of a demand deposit, zero maturity. Bank assets are generally *less* liquid than bank liabilities. The bank offers its deposit customers a *highly* liquid account, relative to the liquidity of the loans it makes.

CHAPTER 12
THRIFT INSTITUTIONS

I. SURVEYING THE TERRITORY: AN AERIAL VIEW

Now, let's be honest. How many of us say we're "going to the bank," when, in fact, we are *really* stopping at the **credit union**? Or, for that matter… how many of us make that little trip without even recognizing that we're in something called a **thrift institution**? Thrift institutions take in deposits and make loans. They're just like commercial banks in that regard (see Chapter 11). In fact, they seem *so* similar that many consumers view them as indistinguishable from commercial banks.

So, why bother with a *separate* chapter on thrifts? Well, for one thing, it helps us understand that some rather similar-looking firms have followed different paths to their current places in the overall market landscape. The primary impetus for the savings and lending arrangements found in *thrift institutions* was recognition of a *consumer* need—for example, financing a home purchase. This contrasts with commercial banks' historical roots in serving *business* borrowing needs. And, even to this day, the balance sheets of thrifts and commercial banks reflect their different histories.

So, when we talk about thrifts versus commercial banks: clearly, they are similar, both being *depository institutions*. But if you go to work for, say, a savings bank, you'll probably be dealing more with household finance than with business finance. One interesting question—which won't be answered here—is whether *both* of these institutional types will survive as *separate* types.

The chapter outline:

Three Categories of Thrift Institutions: Chapter Overview

Savings Associations

Savings Banks

Regulators of Savings Institutions

Savings Associations and Savings Bank Recent Performance

Credit Unions

II.   DIGGING IN THE DIRT: A SUBTERRANEAN VIEW

Key terms

net interest margin
disintermediation
Regulation Q
regulator forbearance
savings association
savings bank
savings institution
DIDMCA
Garn-St. Germain Depository Institutions Act
FIRREA
FDICIA
QTL test
FHLBs
mutual organization
credit union
NCUA
FSLIC
OTS
FDIC
SAIF
BIF
U.S. Central Credit Union
NCUSIF

Got a question?

1. This term is used to refer to either a "savings association" or a "savings bank." This is the: _____.

2. This refers to an "arm" of the FDIC, which insures deposits of savings associations. This is the: _____.

3. This is the chartering agency for federal credit unions. This is the: _____.

4. The _____ were historically referred to as savings and loan associations.

5. The _____ provides deposit insurance for credit union customers.

6. The _____ provides investment and liquidity services to corporate credit union.

7. In a _____the depositors are the legal owners of the institution; no stock is issued.

8. Interest income minus interest expense, divided by earning assets: this is the definition of: _____.

9. This government agency was established in 1989; it charters all federal savings institutions.
   This is: _____.

10. _____ was the federal deposit insurance agency for savings and loan associations until 1989, when it became insolvent and was abolished.

11. The _____ was the federal law passed in 1989, in response to massive failures among savings associations.

12. This refers to a federal regulation, which governed maximum allowable interest rates on deposits, and which became a significant problem for savings institutions in the late 1970s.
    This was: _____.

13. The _____ is a type of depository institution that traditionally was a *mutual organization*, appearing largely in the northeastern United States.

14. There are twelve, government-sponsored _____, which have access to the wholesale capital markets and then lend funds to savings associations.

15. What was behind the declining performance of savings associations in the 1970s and 1980s?

16. Explain the "contentious issue" between credit unions and commercial banks.

17. Explain why, historically, a *negatively sloped yield curve* would provide a serious threat to savings institutions.

18. Contrast the asset holdings of credit unions with the asset holdings of savings institutions.

Got a problem?

1. Take a look at the textbook's **Table 12-4** (Selected Indicators for U.S. Savings Institutions). Figure out the relative size of the savings institutions' **equity**—in particular, the equity-to-assets ratio, for 2001 and 1989

2. Refer to the textbook's **Table 12-3** and **Table 12-6**, which present year-end 2001 information for savings associations, savings banks, and credit unions. Find:
   a) The *dollar amount* of total loans made by each of these three institutional types.
   b) Loans, expressed as a percentage of total assets.

III. WASHING UP... AND THE "ABC" AWARDS

A. The EASIEST THING in the chapter

Well, almost everything! It's really not a hard chapter. No hard analytics. No complicated theories. Of course, sometimes "easy" becomes "hard"—only because we take it lightly. So be forewarned!

B. The HARDEST THING in the chapter

This is not real hard, just irritating. Note our earlier list of terms. *Lots* of them are mere bunches of letters! It's like having the ballplayers identified only by their initials—which is just fine if you go to the ballpark every day. But, why is it this way? Well, it's mostly the result of changing laws and governmental bodies in the 1980s and thereafter. With so many long titles, folks decided to shorten them... to "acronym size." Trouble is, some of the acronyms can be rough on the tongue. (Just how *do* you say DIDMCA?)

C. The FUNNIEST THING in the chapter... or not

We need serious help here. (Or, let's say *not-so-serious* help.) What could possibly be funny about legal and regulatory changes? Or failing savings associations? Let's just leave you with one simple statement...a statement often rolled out in the midst of explanations of the savings and loan crisis of the 1980s...and one that just might capture the essence of incentive problems with deposit insurance:

"Heads I win, tails you lose."

IV.   CHECKING THE ANSWERS...FOR SECTION II

Terms:
1. savings institution
2. SAIF
3. NCUA
4. savings associations
5. NCUSIF
6. U.S. Central Credit Union
7. mutual organization
8. net interest margin
9. OTS
10. FSLIC
11. FIRREA
12. Regulation Q
13. savings bank
14. FHLBs

Essays:
15. Savings associations were in the business of "borrowing short and lending long." And "long" meant *really* long... as in 30-year fixed rate mortgages. The maturities of their assets and liabilities were extremely mismatched, which created a lot of interest rate risk. When market interest rates became high (and volatile) in the late 1970s and early 1980s, these institutions were in trouble. They had to pay higher rates for funding, but were stuck with fixed-rate mortgage portfolios. In addition, Regulation Q meant that they were constrained in terms of what they could pay depositors. So, they suffered from the phenomenon of "disintermediation," as depositors withdrew funds and sought higher interest rates elsewhere.

16. Credit unions are "non-profit" institutions, and therefore enjoy a tax exemption— an exemption deemed to be unfair by commercial bankers. Although credit unions and commercial banks do not offer precisely the same array of services, they do compete for depositor funds, and for consumer loan business.

17. A negatively-sloped yield curve means that short-term rates are higher than long-term rates. An institution in the business of borrowing short-term funding, and then investing in long-term assets, will have problems. Loan revenue may be insufficient to cover interest rate expenses.

18. Savings institutions are heavily involved in home mortgage lending. Credit unions have traditionally been involved in consumer loans outside of the mortgage area—although credit unions are now participating in mortgage lending as well.

Problems:

1. Although the equity-to-assets ratio is not in the table, we can *derive* it from figures that *are* in the table. In particular, note that return on assets (ROA) is simply net income/total assets. Likewise, return on equity (ROE) is net income/total equity. So,

$$\frac{ROA}{ROE} = \frac{\dfrac{NI}{Assets}}{\dfrac{NI}{Equity}} = \frac{Equity}{Assets}$$

Plugging in the numbers for 2001 and 1989:

$$\text{In 2001: } \frac{ROA}{ROE} = \frac{1.08\%}{12.73\%} = \frac{Equity}{Assets} = 8.48\%$$

$$\text{In 1989: } \frac{ROA}{ROE} = \frac{-0.39\%}{-8.06\%} = \frac{Equity}{Assets} = 4.84\%$$

Note the *negative* ROA and ROE figures in 1989—clearly, this was not the best of times for savings institutions. And note how slim the equity-to-assets ratio was, in comparison to the 2001 figure.

2. The only puzzle here might be: where exactly are the loans? Look amidst the assets. And leave aside the securities.

   a) From **Table 12-3**:

	Savings associations	Savings banks
Mtg. Loans	$530,594 million	$227,801 million
Commercial loans	24,550	12,204
Consumer loans	56,128	13,293
Other loans, leases	3,926	3,044
Total loans	$615,198 million	$256,342 million

   From **Table 12-6**:

Home mortgages	$144.2 billion
Consumer credit	186.2
Total loans	$330.4 billion

   Clearly, the credit unions' loan amount is small when compared the numbers for savings institutions (although be sure to distinguish between figures in *millions* and *billions*).

b) Simply divide the figures in part (a) by the relevant *total asset* figures.

Savings associations: $\dfrac{\$615,198}{\$905,632} = 67.9\%$

Savings banks: $\dfrac{\$256,342}{\$393,377} = 65.2\%$

Credit unions: $\dfrac{\$330.4}{\$505.5} = 65.4\%$

CHAPTER 13
DEPOSITORY INSTITUTIONS' FINANCIAL STATEMENTS AND ANALYSIS

I. SURVEYING THE TERRITORY: AN AERIAL VIEW

While Chapters 11 and 12 scanned the depository landscape from a rather high altitude, Chapter 13 digs around at ground level—examining details of the financial statements. Readers with backgrounds in financial statement analysis have a clear edge here. (Yes, accountants, we're talking about *you*.) Much of the terminology will not be new to you. But, even financial statement wizards should stay alert. While depository financial statements certainly include the *usual suspects*—the income statement and the balance sheet—the *form and content* just don't look like those of "XYZ Manufacturing Corp." And why is that?

Well, the depositories aren't in the business of selling steel beams, strawberry ice cream, or spreadsheet programs. Instead, the banks are selling… hmm… what *are* they selling? Simply put, banks buy and sell a whole lot of "paper assets"—or, more formally, *financial assets*. Bottom line: the statements in this industry look a bit different.

Chapter topics:

Why Evaluate Performance of Depository Institutions: Chapter Overview

Financial Statements of Commercial Banks

Financial Statement Analysis Using a Return on Equity Framework

Impact of Market Niche and Bank Size on Financial Statement Analysis

II. DIGGING IN THE DIRT: A SUBTERRANEAN VIEW

Key terms

As you can see...there is no shortage of terms in this chapter...

CAMELS	up-front fee
report of condition	back-end fee
report of income	letters of credit
retail bank	standby letters of credit
wholesale bank	when issued securities
correspondent bank	loans sold
investment securities	recourse
secured loan	derivative securities
unsecured loan	trust services
unearned income	interest income
allowance for loan and lease	interest expense
losses	net interest income
net write offs	provision for loan losses
earning assets	noninterest income
NOW account	noninterest expense
MMDAs	total operating income
retail CDs	extraordinary items
wholesale CDs	net income
negotiable instrument	time series analysis
brokered deposits	cross sectional analysis
borrowed funds	net interest margin
federal funds	spread
repo (or RP)	overhead efficiency
commercial paper	ROA
core deposits	ROE
purchased funds	EM
loan commitment	profit margin
equity capital	asset utilization (AU)

Got a question?

1. Actual loan and lease losses, less the recoveries on loans and leases, are referred to as _____. This is deducted from the allowance for loan and lease losses.

2. Banks offer _____, which are fixed maturity instruments, having face values under $100,000.

3. The _____ is simply another term for the "balance sheet."

4. A _____ is a type of institution that focuses more on *business* banking relationships, rather than consumer banking needs.

5. This is a term for the more "stable" types of deposits—generally encompassing demand deposits, NOW accounts, MMDAs, other savings accounts, and retail CDs.
   These types are called: _____

6. The _____ is the bank's interest income less its interest expenses.

7. Under the system adopted by the Federal Financial Institutions Examination Council, each financial institution's is evaluated on six components of financial condition and operations and assigned a _____ rating.

8. This is a type of deposit account, designed to be competitive with money market mutual funds.
   These are: _____ .

9. _____ have a minimum denomination of $100,000, and they are negotiable instruments.

10. This expense item on the bank's income statement records the current period's allocation to the allowance for loan and lease losses
    This is: _____ .

11. One source of "borrowed funds" for a banking firm is _____ .
    This cannot be issued by a bank subsidiary itself, but a parent bank holding company can issue it, and then "downstream" the funds to the bank.

12. If you subtract the average cost of interest-bearing deposits from the average yield of earning assets you have the: _____ .

13. This term is simply "shorthand" for a repurchase agreement.
    This is: _____ .

14. The _____ expresses net income as a percentage of stockholders' equity.

15. This is an abbreviation for a particular balance sheet ratio—the total assets divided by stockholders' equity.
    This is the: _____

16. With this kind of review, the analyst is making comparisons of one firm's financial statements with those of other firms.
    This is: _____.

17. One asset category on a bank's balance sheet is _____, which includes things like U.S. Treasury, municipal, and mortgage-backed securities. They generate some income for the bank, and are used for liquidity risk management purposes.

18. A bank's _____ consists mainly of preferred stock, common stock, paid-in capital, and retained earnings.

19. _____ refers to wholesale CDs, obtained through a brokerage or investment house, rather than directly from a customer.

20. _____ and _____ are sold by banks to other firms. With both, the bank guarantees to underwrite performance of a firm—such guaranteeing the firm's payment for goods. The latter category covers potentially more severe and less predictable contingencies.

21. A bank will generally find greater yields on its loans than on its security investments. Then, why does the bank bother to hold securities at all?

22. Distinguish the **net interest margin** from the **spread**. And, can you conceive of any special circumstances that would make the two things *equal* to each other?

23. One kind of "off balance sheet" activity is the **loan commitment**.
    a) Explain the nature of such activity. Does such activity ever have "on" balance sheet consequences?
    b) What risk does the bank face when making such a commitment?
    c) How is the bank compensated for such activity?

Got a problem?

1. South Bank has total assets of $16 billion total stockholders' equity of $1 billion. Its ROA is 1.2%. What is its **ROE**?

2. Refer again to South Bank (preceding problem). What is the bank's **net income**?

3. Pacific Bank has total liabilities of $9.6 billion, and stockholders' equity of $0.8 billion. What is Pacific Bank's **equity multiplier**?

4. Western State Bank has the following financial data:

Net income:	$ 90 million
Total assets:	$8,070 million
Earning assets:	$7,000 million
Total stockholders' equity:	$ 500 million
Interest income:	$ 490 million
Interest expense:	$ 180 million

   Compute Western State Bank's:
   a) Equity multiplier.
   b) ROA.
   c) Net interest margin.

5. First National Bank has an ROE of 19%. Last National Bank has an ROE of 24%. Both banks have an ROA of 1.5%. What can we say about the leverage of these banks? And what is the significance of this?

For **problems 6 through 9**, consider North Winds Bank's financial statements:

North Winds Income Statement (in millions)

Interest and fees on loans	$ 605
Interest on security investments	165
Total interest income	$ 770
Total interest expense	$ 390
Provision for loan losses	50
Service charges	140
Other noninterest income	90
Total noninterest income	$ 230
Salaries and employee benefits	220
Other noninterest expense	190
Total noninterest expense	$ 410
Income before taxes	150
Taxes	30
Net income	$ 120

North Winds Balance Sheet (in millions)

Assets:

Cash and due from banks	$ 320
Investments in securities	2,300
Loans	4,510
Premises & fixed assets	70
Total Assets	$7,200

Liabilities & Equity:

Demand deposits	$ 370
NOW accounts	80
MMDAs	1,290
Retail CDs & other savings	3,940
Wholesale CDs	560
Federal funds purchased	340
Total Liabilities	$6,580
Common stock	$ 208
Surplus & Paid-in Capital	135
Retained earnings	277
Total Stockholders' Equity	$ 620
Total Liabilities & Stock. Equity	$ 7,200

6. Compute the following, for North Winds Bank (clue: you'll be working with just *one* of the statements).
   a) The equity multiplier
   b) The core deposits
   c) The earning assets

7. Compute the following, for North Winds Bank (clue: you'll be working with *both* statements).
   a) The ROA
   b) The ROE
   c) The net interest income
   d) The net interest margin
   e) The spread
   f) The interest income ratio
   g) The noninterest income ratio
   h) The asset utilization ratio
   i) The profit margin
   j) The overhead efficiency ratio

8. How could we express North Winds' **ROA** as a function of two other ratios? (Clue: look at text Figure 13-5.)

9. How could we express North Winds' **ROE** as a function of two other ratios? (Clue: look at text Figure 13-5.)

Web cruising ideas

1. So, you want to see some *real* income statement and balance sheet numbers? One obvious thing to do: call up a bank and ask for a statement. Of course, going to the bank's web site has become a more common way—avoiding the necessity of actually speaking with a human being (is it really *that* bad a thing?).

    But you can also get the quarterly "call reports," as filed with bank regulators. Go to the following web site, and *call up* the ones you want. (Thrift institution financial reports are accessible here as well.)

    http://www2.fdic.gov/call_tfr_rpts/

2. If you are more interested in **bank holding company** data—rather than the individual, subsidiary banks—try this site:

    http://www.ffiec.gov/NIC/default.htm

    This is the National Information Center's site, maintained by the Federal Reserve System. You will find size and performance information for bank holding companies, as well as some individual bank information.

III.   WASHING UP... AND THE "ABC" AWARDS

A. The EASIEST THING in the chapter

That's simple. The easiest thing here is *leafing* through the pages...quickly... even *more* quickly... trying to see if there *might* be *something* easy ... somewhere....
(Well, maybe we'll find something easy in the *next* chapter!)

B. The HARDEST THING in the chapter

The hardest thing is wading through tables of income statement and balance sheet numbers, gazing at financial ratios, and then, trying to get some idea about *interpreting* all this. In other words, the hard thing is *everything*. (And yes, dear *wizards* of financial statement analysis, we know you *disagree* with this assessment... but you don't have to *gloat* about it!)

C. The FUNNIEST THING in the chapter... or not

What's the funniest thing? How about this: got a favorite acronym? (Well okay... a favorite somewhere in *Chapter 13*.) Mine's right there at the beginning: CAMELS.
And I often wonder, when confronted with such acronyms: did they *start* with the letters—the **C** in *Capital*, the **A** in *Assets*, etc.—or did some bank regulator *really like* that picture on his favorite tobacco product, and work backwards?

Something else I find amusing... but only after reflecting on *so many* numbers in *so many* bank financial statements. It's the *forest*, which might be getting lost amidst all the concern for *trees*.

Huh?

Let's say you're a bank stockholder. What do you really *care about*—in your role as a stockholder, that is? Did somebody say ROE? And somebody else said ROA? ....
Maybe even a few votes for net interest margin, or the spread? All these ratios are very nice, very interesting. But here's the issue: how do such *ratios* relate to one of your most prized possessions? ... *No, not your Game-Boy...* how do they relate to your *bank stock*? As a stockholder, aren't you concerned with the *value* of those shares?

The point: as bank stockholders, we should care about financial ratios (the *trees*) if they tell us something about our share *value* (the *forest*). And frankly, exactly how the financial ratios *feed into* shareholder value may seem a little fuzzy at times.
(Yes... your *Study Guide* author is very easily amused.)

IV.   CHECKING THE ANSWERS...FOR SECTION II

Terms:
1. net write offs
2. retail CDs
3. report of condition
4. wholesale bank
5. core deposits
6. net interest income
7. CAMELS
8. MMDAs (money market deposit accounts)
9. wholesale CDs
10. provision for loan losses
11. commercial paper
12. spread
13. repo (or RP)
14. ROE (or return on equity)
15. EM (or equity multiplier)
16. cross sectional analysis
17. investment securities
18. equity capital
19. brokered deposits
20. letters of credit; standby letters of credit

Essays:
21. The investment in securities helps the bank maintain sufficient *liquidity*, while not entirely giving up income. Granted, the securities, as a rule, won't be earning what the loans will earn. But the securities are a whole lot more liquid. They can be turned into cash more easily—if there is unanticipated loan demand, or unanticipated deposit outflow.

22. These two terms are closely related. **Net interest margin** is the result of dividing net interest income by earning assets. Now remember that the net interest income is simply interest income minus interest expense. Well, the **spread** incorporates interest income and interest expense, too. But, we first express the interest income as a fraction of earning assets (an earnings rate), and the interest expense as a fraction of interest-bearing liabilities (a cost rate). Then, subtract the latter from the former. If we had a very special set of circumstances—if the earning assets just happened to equal the interest-bearing liabilities—then net interest margin would be equal to the spread.

23. Loan commitments.
   a) When the bank makes a loan commitment, it agrees to lend for a certain period of time, and under certain terms and conditions. It is providing (or selling) a valuable option to the customer. The customer can "take down" the funds when needed—within the bounds of the loan commitment agreement.
   b) The bank does not know precisely when (or if) the funds will be taken by the customer. But the bank has committed itself to provide the funds, even if market conditions have changed.
   c) The bank will often charge an up-front commitment fee for the loan commitment. There could also be back-end fees—perhaps a fee at the time the funds are taken, or possibly a fee based on the unused portion of the commitment.

Problems:

1. $ROE = ROA \times \dfrac{Assets}{Equity} = 1.2\% \times \dfrac{\$16}{\$1} = 19.2\%$

2. Since net income is the numerator of ROA:
$$Net\ income = ROA\ X\ (Total\ Assets)$$
$$= 1.2\%\ X\ \$16\ billion$$
$$= \$0.192\ billion\ (or\ \$192\ million)$$

3. This seems simple enough: after all, the equity multiplier is just Total Assets/Equity. But what *is* the total assets figure? Just sum up total liabilities and equity. So,
$$EM = \dfrac{\$9.6 + \$0.8}{\$0.8} = 13$$

4. These are fairly straight-ahead:
   a) $EM = \dfrac{Assets}{Equity} = \dfrac{\$8,070}{\$500} = 16.14$

   b) Just net income over total assets, or:
   $$ROA = \dfrac{\$90}{\$8,070} = 1.12\%$$

   c) For net interest margin (NIM), first take interest income less the interest expense. Then divide by earning assets:

   $$NIM = \dfrac{\$490 - \$180}{\$7,000} = 4.43\%$$

5. ROE and ROA are "linked" to the equity multiplier (EM). In particular, note that ROE = ROA X EM. So, we can solve to find each bank's equity multiplier.
   <u>First National</u>: 19% = 1.5% X EM, and so, EM = 12.67
   <u>Last National</u>: 24% = 1.5% X EM, and so, EM = 16.00

   Remember that EM = Assets/Equity. So, Last National, with its higher EM, has relatively less equity—and hence, it is using more financial leverage. In general, this would suggest a somewhat riskier capital structure. Creditors (especially those who do not have the benefit of deposit insurance) and bank regulators will be concerned with the leverage of a bank.

6. All these involve just the balance sheet:
   a) Equity multiplier: $7,200/$620 = 11.61 (*not* a percentage!)
   b) Core deposits will encompass the more stable deposit sources: here, take everything except wholesale CDs and federal funds purchased, or $5,680.
   c) For earning assets, think of all the stuff that pays interest, or security investments and loans. In particular, $2,300 + $4,510 = $6,810.

7. Using the given balance sheet and income statement data:
   a) ROA = $120/$7,200 = 1.67%
   b) ROE = $120/$620 = 19.35%
   c) Net interest income is interest income less interest expense:
      $770 − $390 = $380
   d) Divide net interest income (preceding part) by earning assets:
      $380/$6,810 = 5.58%
   e) Spread = yield on earning assets − cost rate on interest bearing deposits.
      Here, yield on earning assets = 770/6810 = 11.31%
      Cost rate on interest bearing deposits = 390/6210 = 6.28%
      Spread = 11.31% - 6.28% = 5.03%
   f) Interest income ratio: divide interest income by total assets.
      $$\frac{\$770}{\$7,200} = 10.69\%$$
   g) Noninterest income ratio: divide noninterest income by total assets.
      $$\frac{\$230}{\$7,200} = 3.19\%$$
   h) Asset utilization (AU): interest and noninterest income, divided by total assets.
      $$\frac{\$770 + \$230}{\$7,200} = 13.89\%$$
   i) Profit margin (PM): net income, divided by total operating income. Note that *total operating income* is what we were just using in the AU ratio—it's the interest income plus noninterest income.
      $$\frac{\$120}{\$770 + \$230} = 12\%$$

j) Overhead efficiency: noninterest income divided by noninterest expense.

$$\frac{\$230}{\$410} = 56.1\%$$

8. ROA can be expressed as the product of the profit margin (PM) and the asset utilization ratio (AU)—both of which we already computed.

$$ROA = PM \times AU = 12\% \times 13.89\% = 1.67\%$$

By the way, did you come up with a number that *seems* to be much larger? If so, recognize that you are multiplying two numbers, both presented here in "percentage clothing." Put the inputs in *decimal* form and you'll see what I'm getting at.

Now, let's check back to part (a), just to make sure we came up with the same answer. (*Yes!* It *is* the same!) This is not a *better* way to compute ROA. No, we're just demonstrating a relationship that *has* to exist.

9. ROE can be expressed as the product of ROA and the equity multiplier (EM)—and again, we already computed them. So,

$$ROE = ROA \times EM = 1.67\% \times 11.61 = 19.35\%$$

And the answer checks with what we came up with in part (b) of problem 7.

CHAPTER 14
REGULATION OF DEPOSITORY INSTITUTIONS

I. SURVEYING THE TERRITORY: AN AERIAL VIEW

So, do you like *long* chapters? Do you like *appendices*? If so, *this is your chapter*!

When it comes to government regulation, many bankers claim they're exposed to *more than* their fair share of it. That's a matter of opinion, of course. But it is fair to say there *are* many rules governing the banking business. And they continue to evolve.

Why *are* banks so heavily regulated? One key thing: remember that a bank relies heavily on *other people's money*. The bank deploys the depositors' money to earn money for the bank's stockholders (and also, of course, for the bankers *hired* by the stockholders). Whenever *other people's money* is involved, there's a question of *how* that money is being used. Will the bank take too much risk with the money, and then break promises to those *other people*—the depositors? Have bank stockholders provided enough of a "cushion," if things go haywire? And if a bank fails, are there larger, negative implications for the economy?

Of course, the word *depositor* isn't synonymous with the word *idiot*—so some observers argue that unfettered markets provide proper incentives for bankers to *do the right thing*. The idea is that if depositors perceive too much risk at "Blue-sky Bank," the bank can lose its funding. Blue-sky's managers know this, so they manage risk appropriately. *Will* free markets provide the right incentives? Or is government intervention necessary? There have been many debates about the proper role of government in the banking industry. This is an important, and deep, issue. And Chapter 14 will not resolve that issue.

But one thing is clear: for many years in the U.S., we've had *significant* governmental presence in banking. We see things like reserve requirements, capital requirements, product limitations, and geographic restrictions. Chapter 14 will give you a feel for how the relationship between banks and government regulators has evolved—the manifestation of the *accepted wisdom* about the role of government in the banking business.

Specialness and Regulation: Chapter Overview

Types of Regulations and the Regulators

Regulation of Product and Geographic Expansion

The History of Bank and Savings Institution Guaranty Funds

Balance Sheet Regulations

Off-Balance-Sheet Regulations

Foreign Versus Domestic Regulation of Depository Institutions

Appendix A: Depository Institutions and Their Regulators

Appendix B: Proposed Changes to the FDIC's Deposit Insurance Premium Assessments

Appendix C: Calculating Minimum Required Reserves at U.S. Depository Institutions

Appendix D: Calculating Risk-Based Capital Ratios

(Appendix material is accessible at: **www.mhhe.com/sc2e.**)

II. DIGGING IN THE DIRT: A SUBTERRANEAN VIEW

Key terms

net regulatory burden
outside money
inside money
QTL test
Regulation Q
Community Reinvestment Act
McFadden Act
Glass-Steagall Act
FIRREA
DIDMCA
FDICIA
Riegle Neal Act
Financial Services
   Modernization Act
universal FI
commercial banking
investment banking
Section 20 affiliate
nonbank bank
de novo office
unit banks
multibank holding company
grandfathered subsidiaries
one-bank holding company
FSLIC

moral hazard
implicit premiums
capital-to-assets ratio
prompt corrective action (PCA)
Basel (or Basle) Accord
risk-adjusted assets
Tier I capital
Tier II capital
Total risk-based capital ratio
Tier I (core) capital ratio
NAFTA
national treatment
cash reserves
transaction accounts
reserve computation period
weekend game
reserve maintenance period
lagged reserve accounting system
contemporaneous reserve
   accounting system
credit equivalent amount
counterparty credit risk
potential exposure
current exposure

Got a question?

1. _____ refers to the activity of underwriting, issuing, and distributing securities.

2. At the beginning of the last century, most U.S. banks were _____.

3. This term refers to a type of institution operating in countries that permit the same institution to offer a broad range of banking and financial services.
This is: _____.

4. In 1988, bank regulators from the U.S. and other member countries of the Bank for International Settlements agreed to implement new risk-based capital ratios for commercial banks.
This agreement is known as the: _____.

5. The term _____ refers to that part of the money supply directly produced by the government or central bank—such as notes and coin.

6. A newly established office is called a: _____.

7. This is a measure of bank capital, which basically includes book value of common equity, plus an amount of perpetual preferred stock, plus minority equity interest held by the bank, less goodwill.
This is: _____.

8. The _____ is the period over which a bank's required reserves are calculated.

9. Passage of the _____ allowed for "financial services holding companies," which could engage in banking activities and securities underwriting.

10. This refers to a legal and regulatory policy, which treats foreign banks in the same way as domestic banks.
This is: _____.

11. A _____ is a securities subsidiary of a bank holding company; its name refers to a provision of the Glass-Steagall Act.

12. This is a reserve accounting scheme in which the reserve computation period and the reserve maintenance period are overlapped, or closely aligned with each.
This is the: _____.

13. The _____ refers to the risk that the "other party" to a contract—like a forward contract or a swap—will default on the obligation.

14. The _____ is also known as the Banking Act of 1933. It sought to impose a rigid separation between commercial banking and investment banking.

15. An example of an asset restriction on depositories is the _____, which requires savings institutions to hold at least 65 percent of their assets in residential mortgage-related assets.

16. The _____ is an example of consumer protection regulation, designed to prevent discrimination by lending institutions.

17. For many years, _____ insured the deposits of savings institutions in the U.S. By 1989, its insurance fund was depleted.

18. The _____ was a law passed in 1980. It started a phase-out of deposit interest rate ceilings, and introduced uniform reserve requirements for state and nationally chartered banks.

19. In reference to the Glass-Steagall Act of 1933:
    a) What did the Act effectively "separate"?
    b) What were the "exemptions" allowed under the law?

20. The Financial Services Modernization Act of 1999 extended the array of financial services that could be provided "under one roof," through a financial services holding company. How are the various activities to be regulated, under this law?

21. Distinguish the "leverage ratio" from a "risk-based capital ratio."

22. How might "moral hazard" have contributed to depository institution problems and the eventual insolvency of FSLIC in the 1980s?

23. What are the *shortcomings* of using the simple capital-to-assets ratio (or "leverage ratio") to assess the soundness of a bank? What alternative is suggested?

Got a problem?

For **problems 1-4**, refer to the following information:

	Bank X (millions)	Bank Y (millions)
Tier I (Core) Capital	$ 136	$ 380
Tier II Capital	37	91
Total Assets	$3,020	$7620
Risk-adjusted assets	$2,680	$4520

1. Compute the "leverage ratios" for Bank X and Bank Y

2. Compute the "total risk-based capital ratios" for Bank X and Bank Y

3. Compute the "Tier I risk-based capital ratios" for Bank X and Bank Y

4. Given your answers to problems 1-3, apply the textbook's Table 14-5 (Specification of Capital Categories...) to Banks X and Y.

For problems **5 and 6**, consider the following bank balance sheet (and if it looks a bit familiar, we used it before, in the preceding chapter):

Assets:	(in millions)
Cash and due from banks	$ 320
Investments in securities	2,300
Loans	4,510
Premises & fixed assets	70
Total Assets	$7,200

Liabilities & Equity:	
Demand deposits	$ 370
NOW accounts	80
MMDAs	1,290
Retail CDs & other savings	3,940
Wholesale CDs	560
Federal funds purchased	340
Total Liabilities	$6,580
Common stock	$ 208
Surplus & Paid-in Capital	135
Retained earnings	277
Total Stockholders' Equity	$ 620
Total Liabilities & Stock. Equity	$ 7,200

5. Compute the bank's **core capital ratio** (or "leverage ratio").

6. Now, let's address the **Tier I risk-based capital ratio.** (We'll use the "Basel II" rules, and assume there are no off-balance sheet items. Refer to **Appendix D** for the Basel II risk categories.) **Compute the Tier I risk-based capital ratio:**
   a) If the bank's *securities* are all U.S. Treasuries, and its *loans* are all to firms with a credit rating of A+ to A-.
   b) If the bank's *securities* are all U.S. Treasuries, and its *loans* are all to firms with a credit rating of BBB+ to BB-.

For **problems 7 and 8**, refer to the following information (Again, these problems relate to **Appendix D** material.)

Bank Assets (in millions)

Cash	$160
Cash Items in Process of Collection	300
Deposits at Federal Reserve	20
U.S. Treasury securities	350
General obligation municipal bonds	140
Revenue municipal bonds	180
Loan on 1-4 family residential property (first liens)	3,025
Loans to individuals	2,540
Loans to businesses	2,110
Bank premises and equipment	125
Total Assets	$8,950

7. Assuming there are no "off-balance-sheet" items to worry about, compute the **risk-adjusted assets** of the bank, under Basel I (Clue: Check Table 14-D1, found in Appendix D.)

8. Suppose that, in addition to the "on-balance sheet" items above, the bank had the following "off-balance sheet" commitments: (1) $185 million in unused loan commitments, original maturity greater than one year, and (2) $70 in commercial letters of credit. Once again, compute the bank's **risk-adjusted assets**. (Clue: Check Table 14-D5, in Appendix D, on "conversion factors" for off balance sheet items.)

Web cruising ideas

If you really don't believe that capital regulation could be of such worldwide interest, go ahead and check it out for yourself. The Bank for International Settlements has an extensive list of publications, located at the following site:

http://www.bis.org/publ/

III. WASHING UP... AND THE "ABC" AWARDS

A. The EASIEST THING in the chapter

Let's stretch the interpretation here and say it's the *easing* of restrictions on what folks running depository institutions can do in the U.S. (Granted, it may not constitute *ease* on the reader!) Aside from traditional banking, the depository institution ball game now includes securities and insurance... and that's not even counting our evolution into the world of interstate banking. You will probably be hard-pressed to find a suspender-snapping banker admitting that the regulatory *burden* is *less*. But it seems we're devoting more and more attention to what these institutions *can do*, instead of what they *can't*.

B. The HARDEST THING in the chapter

The hardest stuff here is the picky, computational stuff on risk-adjusted capital ratios. A close second would be required reserve computations. What makes it hard? Well, it's not the rationale for such measurement systems. Instead, it's the details, or "bookkeeping" stuff. Both of these topics have been relegated to appendices. (And I suspect that more than a few students—and yes, even some *professors*—are happy about that.)

C. The FUNNIEST THING in the chapter... or not

Pardon me, but don't you think we could come to an agreement on how to spell a *word*? In this case, it's the word so often tossed around amidst discussions of capital standards and international bank regulation. That's right: it's "Basle," as in Basle Accord. Or is it "Basel"? Be darned if I know. Not wanting to offend anybody, our textbook covers both bases—or, should I say, *both Basels!*

I thought I could get to the bottom of this at the web site for the Bank of International Settlements. But guess what? They can't make up their minds either! I will say this: although I didn't keep a tally, I think I saw more cases of "Basel" than "Basle" there.

IV.   CHECKING THE ANSWERS...FOR SECTION II

Terms:

1. investment banking
2. unit banks
3. universal FI
4. Basel (or Basle) accord
5. outside money
6. de novo office
7. Tier I capital
8. reserve computation period
9. Financial Services Modernization Act
10. national treatment
11. Section 20 affiliate
12. contemporaneous reserve accounting system
13. counterparty risk
14. Glass Steagall Act
15. qualified thrift lender (QTL) test
16. Community Reinvestment Act (CRA)
17. FSLIC
18. DIDMCA

Essays:

19. Under Glass-Steagall:
    a) *Investment banking* activities (underwriting, issuing ,and distributing securities) were largely separated from *commercial banking* activities (accepting deposits and making loans)
    b) Banks were allowed underwrite Treasury securities and municipal general obligation bonds, and to deal with private placements of stocks and bonds.

20. Banking activities are to be regulated by the traditional bank regulators (the Fed, the OCC, the FDIC). Securities activities are to be regulated by the SEC. Insurance activities are to be regulated by the various insurance regulators at the state level.

21. The "leverage ratio" is simply the "capital-to-assets" ratio. In the numerator, we take the common equity, perpetual preferred stock, and minority interest in equity of consolidated subsidiaries. The denominator contains total assets. With a risk-based capital ratio, we weight the assets (in the denominator of the ratio) according to risk. More risk is associated with more weight. Currently there are two version of the risk-weighted capital ratio: the Tier I ratio (using a narrower definition of capital) and the total risk-based capital ratio (using a broader definition of capital).

22. One view is that depositories took excessive risks, due to a flawed deposit insurance system—a system that did not "price" the insurance for risk. Much of

the institutions' deposit liabilities were covered by federal deposit insurance. Since explicit insurance premiums were not based on risk, institutions might be more willing to "roll the dice" when deploying their funds to various alternative uses. If their riskier choices turned out poorly, then the insurer would be saddled with the losses.

23. In the "assets" part of the capital-to-assets ratio: all assets are not the same in terms of risk. Some—like cash and U.S. Treasury securities—are virtually risk-free. On the other hand, commercial loans can have substantial default risk. A million dollars of commercial loans would therefore naturally require more capital than a million dollars of Treasury securities. But the capital-to-assets ratio does not make adjustments for risk. Turning to the "capital" part of the ratio: some argue that equity capital is a "too narrow" view of capital, if our concern is for the *deposit* liability holders. An alternative to the "capital-to-assets" ratio is to compute a ratio with "risk-adjusted" assets. In other words, use a measurement scheme whereby riskier assets are weighted more heavily. The basic premise is that more capital should be held against riskier assets. So, assets should be "counted" according to their risk contribution.

Problems:

1. Bank X: 136/3020 = 4.50%
   Bank Y: 385/7620 = 5.05%

   The "leverage ratio" is simply the "capital-to-assets" ratio—without making any risk adjustments to the assets.

2. Bank X: (136 + 37)/2680 = 6.45%
   Bank Y: (385 + 91)/7620 = 10.53%

   "Total capital" is simply the Tier I plus the Tier II capital.

3. Bank X: 136/2680 = 5.07%
   Bank Y: 385/4520 = 8.52%

4. Bank X: Leverage ratio—Zone 2 (Adequately capitalized)
           Total risk based—Zone 3 (Undercapitalized)
           Tier I risk based—Zone 2 (Adequately capitalized)

   Bank Y: Leverage ratio—Zone 1 (Well capitalized)
           Total risk based—Zone 1 (Well capitalized)
           Tier I risk based—Zone 1 (Well capitalized)

5. This is just a straight-ahead capital/assets ratio—no risk weighting or "tiers" of anything.
$$\frac{\$620}{\$7,200} = .0861 = 8.61\%$$

6. The Tier I capital is simply the bank's stockholders' equity (see text Table 14-6), or $620. But asset risks—affecting the relevant "risk weights" in Table 14-D3—will make a difference in the risk-based capital ratio:

a) Note that cash and U.S. Treasuries have a zero risk weight. Premises fall in Category 4 in Table 14-D3 (*real* assets)—thereby having 100% weight. Loans to A+ down to A- companies are in Category 3, carrying 50% weight. So,

$$\frac{\$620}{(\$320\times 0\%)+(\$2,300\times 0\%)+(\$4,510\times 50\%)+(\$70\times 100\%)} = 26.67\%$$

b) The only thing different now is that the loans are more risky—so they are weighted more heavily in the ratio:

$$\frac{\$620}{(\$320\times 0\%)+(\$2,300\times 0\%)+(\$4,510\times 100\%)+(\$70\times 100\%)} = 13.54\%$$

Note that a more risky loan portfolio can make a substantial difference in our ratio measurement.

7. Apply the weights from Table 14-D1 (Appendix D).

Bank Assets (in millions)	Amt.	x Weight	= Risk-wtd.
Cash	$ 160	0	0
Cash Items in Process of Collection	300	.2	20
Deposits at Federal Reserve	20	0	0
U.S. Treasury securities	350	0	0
General obligation municipal bonds	140	.2	28
Revenue municipal bonds	180	.5	90
Loan on 1-4 family residential property (first liens)	3,030	.5	1,515
Loans to individuals	2,540	1.0	2,540
Loans to businesses	2,110	1.0	2,110
Bank premises and equipment	125	1.0	125
Total Assets	$8,950		$6,428

8. For the off-balance-sheet stuff, first apply the relevant "conversion factors" to determine the credit equivalent amounts (refer to Table 14-D5):

Loan commitments: $190 x .5 = $85
Comm. letters of credit: $70 x .2 = $14

Next, apply the risk weights—in this case 100% or 1.0. So the risk-weighted asset figure for the off-balance-sheet items would be ($85 + $14) x 1.0 = $99.

Finally, the *total* risk-weighted asset computation:
$6,428 (on balance sheet)
+ 99 (off balance sheet)
$6,527 total risk-weighted assets

CHAPTER 15
INSURANCE COMPANIES

I.   SURVEYING THE TERRITORY: AN AERIAL VIEW

The outline for this chapter is pretty simple. There are two broad categories of insurance: life and property-casualty. Life insurance is pretty much self-explanatory. (But, seriously, shouldn't it be called *death insurance*?) In the property-casualty arena, the policies cover damages to our autos, homes, boats, etc.—as well as losses caused by our liabilities to others. If someone slips on your snowy driveway, for example, you just might be asked to pay medical expenses.

The basic idea behind the insurance business is pretty simple too. Insurance companies allow people to *pool* their risks. Maybe "Jake" faces the risk that his home will burn down. It's not likely to happen, but if a fire *does* occur, the consequences are disastrous. So, Jake likes the idea of paying a little something every year—in return for having his house replaced if it *does* burn down. Of course, there are lots of "Jakes" out there. The insurance company takes that "little something" from many of them, and then pays it out to those few who actually do suffer a loss. The company has to be careful about charging the *right* little something, of course—so there will be enough funding to cover the claims. And, while they're waiting for the next fire to occur, the insurance company invests the funds to earn a little something for itself.

This is an industry in which *information* is incredibly important. Obviously, to charge the right premium on Jake's homeowner's policy, the insurer needs to judge the likelihood of a fire in a large sample of homes—and this requires data. But also, there is an information-related problem that emerges in the business. It occurs when information is not equally- known by all the market participants. Who is *most likely* to call up and apply for an insurance policy? It just might be the person who's aware of a risk—a risk not yet known to the insurance company. The buzzword for this is *adverse selection*. Of course, the insurance company executives *weren't born yesterday*... so they may look upon an *eager* applicant with a suspicious eye.

The major topics in the chapter:

Two Categories of Insurance Companies: Chapter Overview

Life Insurance Companies

Property-Casualty Insurance Companies

II.   DIGGING IN THE DIRT: A SUBTERRANEAN VIEW

Key terms

adverse selection
ordinary life
term life
whole life
endowment life
variable life
universal life
variable universal life
group life
credit life
annuities
private pension funds
accident and health
insurance
policy loan
policy reserves
surrender value of a policy
separate account
McCarran-Ferguson Act

NAIC
insurance guarantee fund
P&C insurance
net premiums written
fire insurance
homeowners multiple peril insurance
commercial multiple peril insurance
automobile liability and physical damage
    insurance
liability insurance
unearned premium
frequency of loss
severity of loss
long-tail loss
loss ratio
premiums earned
combined ratio
operating ratio
underwriting cycle

Got a question?

1. This refers to an item found on the liability side of the balance sheet; it represents the portion of insurance premiums paid *before* the coverage period has started.
   This is the: _____.

2. The actual losses incurred on a policy line, divided by the premiums earned, is called the: _____.

3. Property & casualty insurance companies can face a so-called _____ when a claim is filed long after the insured event occurs, perhaps even after the coverage period has expired.

4. Among property & casualty insurers, the pattern shown by profits in the industry is referred to as the: _____.

5. _____ is a type of life insurance, usually issued to corporate employees, in which a large number of people are insured under a single policy.

6. Unlike traditional life insurance policies that promise to pay the insured the fixed or face amount of a policy, this type of insurance invests the premium payments in mutual funds of stocks, bonds, and money market instruments. The value of the policy changes with the returns of the mutual fund in which premiums are invested.
   This is: _____.

7. On a life insurance company's balance sheet, the _____ category represents loans made to the company's own policyholders, using their policies as collateral.

8. A problem known as _____ arises in insurance, because those who want to buy an insurance policy are often those who are more prone to have a claim against the insurance company.

9. The biggest single item represented on the liability side of the life insurance industry balance sheet is _____, which represents the insurer's expected future commitments to pay out on present contracts.

10. When a P&C company's _____ is less than 100 percent, this means the company is profitable.

11. The _____ was a law passed in 1945, relating to the insurance business. It confirms the primacy of state regulation over federal regulation.

12. The _____ business involves insurance against the loss of real and personal property, as well as against legal liability.

13. Of the four basic categories life insurance, this category accounts for the biggest share of policies. It is comprised of life policies marketed on an individual basis, and includes such sub-categories as term life, whole life, and universal life.
    This is: _____.

14. This is a particular type of life insurance, which combines a pure (or term) insurance element with a savings element. It guarantees a payout to beneficiaries during a certain period. If the insured person lives to a specified time, he/she receives the face amount of the policy.
    This is: _____.

15. The _____ is an association of state insurance commissioners in the U.S. This body developed a coordinated examination system, employed by various state insurance regulatory commissions.

16. In the _____ segment of the life insurance business, funds are invested and held separately from the insurance company's other assets. The payoffs on policies in this business are linked to the assets in which policy premiums are invested.

17. What is the basic structure of the government regulation faced by the insurance industry in the U.S.?

18. The text indicates that *annuities* are the "reverse" of life insurance. Explain.

19. Look over the text's Table 15-5, on property-casualty underwriting ratios. There are some observations going back as far as the 1950s and 1960s, and continuing right up to 2001. Explain what we're seeing over time. What are the implications?

Got a problem?

1. Mary wants to buy an annuity that will pay her $14,000 per year for the rest of her life, with the first payment from the company starting one year from now. The insurance company estimates that Mary will be alive for 38 more years. What is the least amount the insurance company can charge Mary for the annuity, right *now*, if
   a) The company expects to earn 6% annually on its funds?
   b) The company expects to earn 4.5% annually on its funds?

2. Suppose Heather has a life expectancy of 38 years (just like Mary in the preceding problem). She also wants to buy an annuity... but with a key difference: her first payment from the company would be received in exactly 12 years. What is the least amount the insurance company can charge Heather, right *now*, if
   a) The company expects to earn 6% annually on its funds?
   b) The company expects to earn 4.5% annually on its funds?

For **problems 3 and 4**, consider Coverall Property & Casualty Co. It has the following ratios:

Loss ratio	= 75.5%
Expense ratio	= 29.2%
Dividend ratio	= 1.5%

In addition, the company's net investment income divided by premiums earned was 9.5%

3. Compute the Coverall's *combined ratio* (after dividends).

4. Compute Coverall's *operating ratio*. Further, what if Coverall's net investment income fell to 4.5% of premiums? What would happen to Coverall's operating ratio? What could we say about Coverall's *profitability*?

Web cruising ideas

1. We know the insurance industry is regulated at the *state* level. One good resource is the National Association of Insurance Commissioners (NAIC)—basically, it's a consortium of the various state regulators. You can find them at the following web site:

   http://www.naic.org/splash.htm

2. Let's say you want to know who to contact about insurance regulation in Wyoming. Well, the NAIC has a nice map laid out for you:

   http://www.naic.org/1regulator/usamap.htm

3. And, oh yeah, what about Wyoming? Try this site:

   http://insurance.state.wy.us/

III.   WASHING UP... AND THE "ABC" AWARDS

A. The EASIEST THING in the chapter

The basic idea that motivates this business makes sense to most people. This is a business that clearly reminds us of the *aversion* people have to *risk*. Folks are willing to *pay* to avoid risk. That's the premise of the whole business.

B. The HARDEST THING in the chapter

We've all seen balance sheets and income statements before, but the statements of the life insurance and property-casualty insurance industries can be a bit puzzling. Just keep in mind that this is a business in which paper "promises" are sold... and then the proceeds are used to buy other promises (e.g., securities).

C. The FUNNIEST THING in the chapter... or not

Ever go to the movies? Well, when the subject is insurance, the first thing that comes to my mind is an early Woody Allen movie, *Take the Money and Run*. Okay, let me explain...

Woody plays a down-on-his-luck guy, and at one point, he finds himself in movieland's stereotypical southern prison. For prisoners needing a bit of, shall we say... extra *motivation*...there's the dreaded *hot box*—a small, wooden shack, out in the middle of the prison yard. It's an oven. And one built for punishment.

Well, you know where Woody ends up. But he's not just locked up to do his hard time alone. No, it's worse than that. *Much* worse. Woody has to spend his 24 hours in the hot box with... *an insurance salesman*!

I know, I know... the insurance company reps in the audience aren't laughing. But the movie tapped into a very real, human reaction to insurance companies. Why such a reaction? I'm not sure. Perhaps it's fear of the *hard sell*. Or, maybe it's the nature of the insurance contract itself. You buy something, hoping the insurer never has to pay off!   And if a claim *is* made... well, it's probably in unpleasant circumstances. We really don't hate insurance companies...well, *not everybody does*, ... but perhaps we dislike the fact that they remind us of difficult situations.

IV. CHECKING THE ANSWERS...FOR SECTION II

Terms:
1. unearned premium
2. loss ratio
3. long-tail loss
4. underwriting cycle
5. group life
6. variable life
7. policy loans
8. adverse selection
9. policy reserves (see the text's Table 15-2)
10. operating ratio
11. McCarran-Ferguson Act
12. P&C insurance (for "Property & Casualty")
13. ordinary life
14. endowment life
15. NAIC (for National Association of Insurance Commissioners)
16. separate account

Essays:
17. The U.S. insurance industry is regulated at the *state level*, and the primacy of the state governments in insurance regulation is affirmed in the McCarran-Ferguson Act of 1945. There is also no federally sponsored insurance for the insurance industry, as there is for the depository institution industry (e.g., FDIC).

18. With a typical ordinary life policy, you make a series of payments to the company. Then, upon death, there is a payout from the company (or there could be a payment back to you before death, with an endowment policy). In contrast, if you buy an annuity, you pay for the right to *receive* a series of payments in the future.

19. The combined ratio (and the combined ratio after dividends) is over 100 in most of the reported years. In fact, for the combined ratio after dividends, the only reported years when the ratio was below 100 appear in the first two lines of the table (1951 and 1960). The ratios were especially high in 2000 and 2001. Greater investment income would have been required for the firms to show profitability in such years.

Problems:

1. Simply compute the present value of the 38 payments, discounting at the relevant interest rate. As a practical matter, this can be done with a financial calculator, with a spreadsheet program, or with a "present value of an annuity" table.

    a) Here is the "long way" to represent the problem:

    $$PV = \frac{\$14{,}000}{(1.06)} + \frac{\$14{,}000}{(1.06)^2} + \frac{\$14{,}000}{(1.06)^3} + \cdots + \frac{\$14{,}000}{(1.06)^{38}} = \$207{,}844.27$$

    With an annuity table set-up:

    $$PV = PMT \times PVIFA_{i,n}$$
    $$PV = \$14{,}000 \times PVIFA_{6\%,38}$$
    $$PV = \$14{,}000 \times 14.846 = \$207{,}844$$

    And, of course, many of you are using financial calculators—which basically means that the PVIFA is already "in the machine" for you.

    b) At the 4.5% rate:

    $$PV = \frac{\$14{,}000}{(1.045)} + \frac{\$14{,}000}{(1.045)^2} + \frac{\$14{,}000}{(1.045)^3} + \cdots + \frac{\$14{,}000}{(1.045)^{38}} = \$252{,}844.27$$

2. Now the problem has changed to a *two-stage* one. First, get the present value of an annuity having 27 payments—or, 38 less 11. *Note*: since the payments are to start in exactly 12 years, that means eleven *fewer* payments than in the preceding problem. Second, recognize that *the first stage* present value is really a value *eleven* years in the future—so "bring it back" *eleven* more years.

    a) First, with a 6% discount rate.

    First stage:
    $$PV = PMT \times PVIFA_{i,n}$$
    $$PV = \$14{,}000 \times PVIFA_{6\%,27}$$
    $$PV = \$14{,}000 \times 13.2105 = \$184{,}947$$

    Second stage: Recognize that the "PV" above is actually a value eleven years in the future. So, treat it as a future value (FV) and bring it back to *now*.

    $$PV = \frac{\$184{,}947}{(1.06)^{11}} = \$97{,}428$$

b) Now use 4.5%.

$$PV = \$14,000 \times PVIFA_{4.5\%,27}$$
$$PV = \$14,000 \times 15.4513 = \$216,318.24$$

$$PV = \frac{\$216,318.24}{(1.045)^{11}} = \$133,295.03$$

3. The combined ratio (after dividends):
   $$75.5 + 29.2 + 1.5 = 106.2$$

4. The operating ratio:
   = Combined ratio after dividends – investment yield
   = 106.2 - 9.5
   = 96.7

   If the return on the premiums ("investment yield") fell to 4.5%, the combined ratio would be 101.7. Bottom line: Coverall's expenses would be overwhelming its premium and investment income—it would be unprofitable.

CHAPTER 16
SECURITIES FIRMS AND INVESTMENT BANKS

I. SURVEYING THE TERRITORY: AN AERIAL VIEW

We turn now to firms involved in things like *brokering*, *dealing*, and *underwriting* securities. The activities basically involve accommodating various customers: either folks who need funds, or folks looking to invest their funds. One customer might be a firm wanting to offer new shares of stock. Another might be an individual, desiring to unload some securities and reinvest the money elsewhere.

It may be useful to reflect for a moment, and put Chapter 16's coverage into a larger context. In the last few chapters, we've been examining the *depository institutions* (those *Bank Ones* of the world) and the *insurance companies* (the *Aetnas*). Now, we turn to *Merrill Lynch*, *Goldman Sachs*, and many more. We see detail upon detail... a virtual mountain of features that distinguish these firms. But still, just like depositories, these firms are dealing with "paper" stuff—or financial *claims*. Claims are sold to customers— showing up on the right-hand side of the *seller's* balance sheet. At the same time, those claims show up on the left-hand side of some *buyer's* balance sheet. And the various financial service firms have important roles to play in the process, accommodating the funds-flow from suppliers to the ultimate users.

In fact, organizing our discussion by *type of firm* is a bit misleading. Bank holding companies, for example, conducted *some* underwriting activities for many years—despite the Glass-Steagall Act. Then, in 1999, the Financial Services Modernization Act enabled even more movement by financial firms beyond their traditional boundaries. Now, one corporation can be dabbling in deposit-taking, lending, selling insurance, and underwriting securities. Although we still speak of *commercial banks*, *insurance companies* and *investment banks*—it turns out that the real breakdown is by *function or activity*.

The major chapter topics:

Services Offered by Securities Firms versus Investment Banks: Chapter Overview

Size, Structure, and Composition of the Industry

Securities Firm and Investment Bank Activity Areas

Recent Trends and Balance Sheets

Regulation

Global Issues

II. DIGGING IN THE DIRT: A SUBTERRANEAN VIEW

Key terms

M&As
broker-dealer
underwriting
discount broker
investment banking
private placement
public offering
best efforts underwriting
firm commitment underwriting
underwriting spread
market making
agency transactions
principal transactions
position trading
pure arbitrage
risk arbitrage
program trading
stock brokerage
electronic brokerage
cash management account (CMA)
SEC
NSMIA of 1996
Corporate governance and accounting oversight bill
Rule 144A
Rule 415
shelf registration

Got a question?

1. _____ is a general term, referring to the activities of underwriting and distributing new issues of debt and equity securities.

2. In a public offering of new securities, one possible arrangement is a _____, in which investment bankers act as agents on a fee basis related to their success in placing a new issue of securities with investors.

3. _____ involves the creation of a secondary market in an asset by a securities firm or investment bank.

4. This type of stockbroker conducts trades for customers, but does not offer investment advice.
   This is the: _____.

5. _____ refers to the trading alternative of using the Internet, and thereby bypassing traditional brokers.

6. One part of the investment banking business is in the corporate finance area, advising companies on _____.

7. Corporations can register new issues with the SEC up to two years in advance.
   This is referred to as: _____.

8. When a securities firm assists customers in the trading of existing securities, it is acting as a: _____.

9. Trading defined by the NYSE as the simultaneous buying and selling of a portfolio of at least fifteen different stocks valued at more than $1 million, and using computer programs to initiate the trades, is referred to as:
   _____.

10. One type of trading activity entails buying an asset in one market at one price and selling it immediately in another market at a higher price.
    This is: _____.

11. This refers to the SEC ruling, governing the boundaries between the *public offering* of securities and the *private placement* of securities.
    This is: _____.

12. With a _____, an investment bank purchases new securities directly from an issuing firm at one price; then the bank offers them to the public at a higher price.

13. The _____ is a deposit-like account, offered to investors by securities firms and investment banks.

14. The _____ was passed in 2002, with the intention of preventing deceptive accounting and management practices. It created an independent auditing oversight board under the SEC, among other things.

15. The difference between the underwriter's buy price and the public offer price is called the _____.

16. In gauging the size of securities firms and investment banks, why does the text use *equity capital*, rather than *asset value*?

17. Contrast *agency transactions* with *principal transactions*.

18. The business of securities underwriting has been affected by a 1987 action of the Federal Reserve and by the Financial Services Modernization Act (1999). Explain.

19. How does the relative size of equity capital for firms in securities industry compare with the equity capital of firms in commercial banking?

Got a problem?

1. Van Landen Corp. is issuing new shares of stock, with Marx & Co. serving in the underwriting role. Marx promises $19 per share to Van Landen, with plans to sell 5 million shares. Marx intends to sell the share to the public for $20 per share.
   a) What is the *underwriting spread*?
   b) What is the maximum gross revenue for Marx & Co.?
   c) If the shares sell as intended, how much will Van Landen receive?

2. Allover Investment Corp. is assisting Walters Corp. in an offering of stock. Ten million shares are to be offered. Allover has agreed to underwrite the issue, paying Walters Corp. $15.50 per share. The shares will be offered to the pubic at $16 per share.
   a) How much will Walters Corp. receive from the new issue, if things go as planned?
   b) What was Allover's underwriting spread, and what is the maximum gross revenue it can receive from the issue?
   c) Suppose the shares sell at an average price of $15.80. What is Allover's actual gross revenue? Also, how much will Walters receive in this situation?

Web cruising ideas

1. There's a wealth of information available at the web site of the Securities Industry Association. One particular page allows you to access a ton of their published information. Go to:

   http://www.sia.com/publications/html/online_publications.html

   Here are a couple of specific things to look for:

   a) Quarterly securities industry financial results—available in an Excel file.
   b) Selected industry statistics—which provides the latest underwriting data.

   (A clue: look for the word *research*.)

2. Aside from looking at *industry* financial data, it may be useful to look at an individual company's financial statements. Goldman Sachs makes their annual report available online. Go to their investor relations page:

   http://www.gs.com/our_firm/investor_relations/index.html

   See if you can dig up their recent earnings—or how about their balance sheet?

III. WASHING UP... AND THE "ABC" AWARDS

A. The EASIEST THING in the chapter

Well, the easiest thing might be the *lack* of a certain something. In particular, this is a chapter that's really *light* when it comes to number-crunching exercises. You can survive this chapter with dead batteries in your calculator!

B. The HARDEST THING in the chapter

Perhaps the hardest thing is staying motivated on industry details, when we know full well that big changes are occurring. For example, the text mentions the advent of electronic brokerage, but this is but a tiny sample of what lies ahead... and not too far down the road, either. Our computer technology has allowed folks to deal *more directly*. Just how far will it all go? Will an individual investor want to buy new shares of stock electronically—perhaps even directly from the issuing firm? Will separate and distinct "middlemen" be a significant part of the landscape, in a world where direct communications are so easy and cheap? Good questions. But as with all prognosticating, we have only tentative answers.

C. The FUNNIEST THING in the chapter... or not

Perhaps the funniest thing is that traditional terminology describing various financial firms seems to be losing its value. An enterprise once described as a *commercial bank* may be doing a lot of Chapter 16's *investment banking* stuff as well.

And, thinking about terminology, I'm reminded of a finance professor who claimed that talking about an "investment bank" was like talking about "Grape Nuts." *Grape Nuts?* A *cereal*? ...Well, they're *not grapes*.... But they're sure as heck *not nuts* either.

Likewise, just a few years ago, when we thought about an investment bank... Well, it's not exactly a *bank*... and it's not exactly doing *investments*.

But now? Well, that same *investment bank* just might be doing *both* banking and investing... and a *whole lot more*.

IV.   **CHECKING THE ANSWERS…FOR SECTION II**

Terms:
1. investment banking
2. best efforts underwriting
3. market making
4. discount broker
5. electronic brokerage
6. M&As (for mergers & acquisitions)
7. shelf registration
8. broker-dealer
9. program trading
10. pure arbitrage
11. Rule 144A
12. firm commitment underwriting
13. cash management account (CMA)
14. corporate governance and accounting oversight board
15. underwriting spread

Essays:
16. Securities trading and underwriting generates does not require that the financial institution actually hold the securities they are trading or issuing for their customers. Consequently, asset size is not the most informative measure of a firm's size in this industry. The trading and underwriting can generate profits, which then will influence the size of equity.

17. Market making can involve agency transactions or principal transactions. Agency transactions are two-way transactions on behalf of customers. The firm may buy stock from one customer, and immediately resell it to another customer. In a principal transaction, the market maker seeks to profit on the price movements of securities. So, for example, a market maker builds or reduces its inventory of a given stock, in anticipation of a price movement.

18. In 1987, the Federal Reserve broadened the underwriting powers allowed for bank holding companies. This meant more competition offered by such firms in the securities business—through the bank holding companies' so-called "section 20 subsidiaries." In 1999, passage of the Financial Services Modernization Act removed Glass-Steagall's barriers and restrictions between commercial banks and investment banks—and this should mean even more competition in the industry.

19. Check year-end balance sheet figures for broker-dealers, reported in text Table 16-7. We see equity capital at 4.28% of assets. This is lower than comparable ratios figures observed in recent years in commercial banking (over 8%). Broker-dealer activity would generally be expected to be less risky, involving the trading of more liquid assets than those found in commercial banking.

Problems:

1. The math is straight forward here.
   a) The underwriting spread: $20 - $19 = $1. (It's just the difference between the public offer price and the underwriter's buy price.)
   b) Marx & Co. will receive $1 X 5 million shares, or $5 million.
   c) Van Lanen will receive $19 X 5 million shares, or $95 million.

2. On the Walters issue:
   a) Walters will receive $15.50 per share, times 10 million, or $155 million.
   b) The difference between the firm commitment price to Walters ($15.50) and the offer price to the public ($16) is $.50 per share—that's the underwriting spread. Multiply this by 10 million shares to get the maximum gross revenue, or $5 million.
   c) Given this scenario, Allover pockets only $.30 per share, resulting in gross revenue of $3 million. But Walters will receive the same amount computed in part (a)--$155 million.

CHAPTER 17
FINANCE COMPANIES

I.   SURVEYING THE TERRITORY: AN AERIAL VIEW

The financial institutions just keep on coming, don't they?

Now, we're dealing with yet another *distinct* institution type. Yet, when you think about it, the particular "products" have been encountered before, in the context of *other* institutions—consumer loans, real estate loans, and business loans. So, what's *different* here? Why is there yet another category—another *institutional form*—supplying the same sort of product?

The clues appear early in the chapter. While some finance company loans are just like those made by a commercial bank, others are geared towards a higher-risk segment of the lending market. Some finance companies probably emerged to handle the special surveillance requirements of a higher-risk customer base. And it's probably no accident that finance companies are *not* depositories. Using consumer-supplied deposits to finance higher-risk assets probably wouldn't make good business sense (and, since taking deposits *and* making loans would put the company into the *banking* business, there would be bank regulators to deal with).

Also, note the text's mention of the first major finance company, General Electric Capital Corp. This suggests another important impetus behind finance companies: manufacturing firms, interested in accommodating their customers' financing needs. And—unless you've been on a desert island for a *long time*—you are fully aware of the financing packages mixed in with the marketing stew served up by Ford or General Motors. Having a captive finance company can make it easier for GM to insert a financing angle into its marketing strategy.

The chapter's major topics:

Finance Company Functions: Chapter Overview

Size, Structure, and Composition of the Industry

Balance Sheet and Recent Trends

Industry Performance

Regulation

Global Issues

II.   DIGGING IN THE DIRT: A SUBTERRANEAN VIEW

Key terms

> **sales finance institution**
> **personal credit institution**
> **business credit institution**
> **factoring**
> **captive finance company**
> **subprime lender**
> **loan shark**
> **securitized mortgage assets**
> **retail motor vehicle loan**
> **wholesale motor vehicle loan**
> **floor plan loan**
> **leasing**
> **electronic lending**
> **regulatory oversight**

Any questions?

1. This is a type of finance company specializing in financing to corporations, especially through equipment leasing and factoring. This is the: _____.

2. A _____ is a finance company specializing in making loans to customers of a specific retailer or manufacturer.

3. A _____ refers to a finance company that lends to high-risk customers.

4. One service offered by finance companies is _____, in which the finance company purchases accounts receivable at a discount from face value, assuming responsibility for collecting the accounts.

5. In the late 1990s, _____ boomed. It allows consumers to find, apply for, and close on personal loans—completely over the Internet.

6. One way in which finance companies have engaged in real estate financing is by purchasing _____, which are securities backed by pools of mortgage loans.

7. Finance companies face limited _____ relative to other firms we have talked about.

8. Some finance companies are subsidiaries of "parent" corporations, and have major role in financing the purchases of the parent corporation's products.
   Such a company is called a: _____.

9. A finance company specializing in making installment and other loans to consumers is called a: _____.

10. A _____ occurs when a finance company finances the inventory of a car dealer—i.e., the loan is from the finance company to the dealer, *not* to the dealer's customers.

11. When a finance company engages in _____, repossession in the event of a default is less complicated, because it retains title to the asset being financed.

12. Why might a finance company find it preferable to *own and lease* equipment to a customer, rather than to finance the customer's *purchase* of the equipment?

13. What are the three basic types of loans provided by finance companies? Based on text statistics from recent years, which area has been most significant?

14. In general, how do rates charged by finance companies on consumer loans compare with those charged by banks? Why? In addition, can you find some statistics in the text that seem to contradict this generalization?

15. How does the "liabilities and equity" portion of the balance sheet for the finance company industry compare with that for commercial banks?

16. In the early 2000s, the state of the U.S. economy had important implications for a lending segment served by some finance companies. Explain.

Got a problem?

1. Pat wants to borrow $12,000 from Fantastik Finance Co. The rate being charge on the loan is 16%, and the loan will be paid off in 36 equal, monthly installments. What is the **monthly payment amount** on Pat's loan?

2. SuperShark Money Shop offers Bill the following deal: a $1,000 loan, to be paid back in 12 monthly installments of $95.83. What is the **annual interest rate** on Bill's loan? (Clue: You're looking for the quoted annual rate on loan—analogous to a yield to maturity on a bond.)

3. Tom needs fifty bucks to hold him over until payday—which is one week from now. George agrees to give him the fifty, provided that Tom will pay him back $55 on payday. Tom agrees. What is the **compounded annual rate** on this deal? (Clue: You're looking for the "equivalent annual rate," discussed earlier in the text.)

Web cruising ideas

It might be fun—okay, let's just say *useful*—to go to the web site of a finance company and look at some financial information. For General Motors' GMAC, go to the following page:

http://www.gmacfs.com/

1. Try to find the statements that GMAC files with the SEC. (Clue: Look for "investing" information.)

2. Next, look into the "debt" category and see if the sources of funding for GMAC seem to "fit" with the generalizations made in our chapter.

III.   WASHING UP… AND THE "ABC" AWARDS

A.   The EASIEST THING in the chapter

One thing is clear: the list of terms in this chapter is *much* shorter. In fact, the chapter as a whole is shorter. Let's hope readers don't feel cheated.

B.   The HARDEST THING in the chapter

Believe it or not… I think we have *finally* come to a chapter where it's kind of *hard* to find really *hard stuff.* The problems are almost non-existent… and merely remind us of the loan payment problems encountered much earlier in the text. The list of terms is short. I rest my case.

C.   The FUNNIEST THING in the chapter… or not

I don't know… but seeing the term *"loan shark"* in the chapter may seem a little peculiar. Most readers will have a pretty good sense for the meaning of the term (did anybody out there really need the textbook's formal definition?). But I just wonder… do you suppose we could find a *list* of these companies? Would there possibly be a trade group, maybe something like the "National Loan Shark Association"? Does the Federal Reserve, in collecting its vast arsenal of financial data, have a separate category called *loan shark lending*?

IV.   CHECKING THE ANSWERS...FOR SECTION II

Terms:
1. business credit institution
2. sales finance institution (and, it could be a *captive* finance company)
3. subprime lender (or, it could be a loan shark)
4. factoring
5. electronic lending
6. securitized mortgage assets
7. regulatory oversight
8. captive finance company
9. personal credit institution
10. wholesale motor vehicle loan (or floor plan loan)
11. leasing

Essays:
12. If the customer runs into trouble and the assets must be "taken back" by the finance company, the legal wrangling is easier with a lease—because the lessor (the finance company here) already *owns* the property. Also, since the finance company owns the property with a lease arrangement, it gets the benefit of writing off the depreciation expense.

13. The three basic types are: (1) real estate loans, (2) consumer loans, and (3) business loans. Business loans (and leasing) have been the largest part of the business recently. In June, 1999, business loans comprised about 49 percent of finance company loans.

14. In general, the text reports that consumer loans extended by finance companies have higher interest rates. The reason would most likely be a higher-risk customer group, on the whole. The apparent "contradictory" piece of evidence is found in Table 17-4, which reports Consumer Credit Interest Rates in recent years. In the most recent years reported—1997 through 1999—rates on loans to finance *new* cars were somewhat higher at commercial banks. This is attributed to efforts of major auto manufacturers, as they responded to slack car demand by cutting financing rates at their affiliated finance companies.

15. On the liability side of commercial bank balance sheet, *deposits* provide the key item. Finance companies do not offer deposit liabilities. Finance companies *borrow* heavily, with much of it attributable to issuance of *commercial paper*. Also, from the June 30, 1999 finance company balance sheet (the text's Table 17-1), the capital accounts amounted to 12.4 percent of total assets—showing relatively higher "book" capitalization than we observed among depository institutions.

16. The U.S. economy experienced a downturn in the early 2000s. Economic downturns present problems for lenders, as borrowers find it difficult to make their payments. This kind of problem was especially pronounced for sub-prime lenders—those who take on higher-risk borrowers. This segment of the business suffered rising delinquencies and losses.

Problems:

1. Here, we are looking for the payment (or PMT) in a *present value of an annuity* equation. We already know the present value—that's $12,000. The per-month interest rate is 16% divided by 12, or 1.333%. So,

$$\$12,000 = PMT \times PVIFA_{1.333\%,36} = PMT \times 28.4438$$

Solving this, we find PMT = $421.88. (Naturally, those using financial calculators are just looking for PMT, rather than fooling around with a PVIFA factor.)

2. Again, we're dealing with equal monthly payments. So again, we're dealing with the *present value of an annuity* equation. Now we have a *different unknown*. **Note:** If you don't use a financial calculator or spreadsheet program, this can be a bit tedious. Below is the basic equation, where PMT = $95.83. You have to find the "i" in the following:

$$\$1,000 = \frac{\$95.83}{\left(1 + \frac{i}{12}\right)} + \frac{\$95.83}{\left(1 + \frac{i}{12}\right)^2} + \ldots + \frac{\$95.83}{\left(1 + \frac{i}{12}\right)^{12}}$$

Or, in PVIFA "clothing":

$$\$1,000 = \$95.83 \times PVIFA_{i/12,12}$$

You can solve for i = 26.62%, with a financial calculator or a spreadsheet program.

3. The five bucks doesn't seem like much, on the surface. But Tom is paying 10% interest *per week*. The equivalent (or "effective") annual rate is going to look downright *ugly*.

$$(1+.10)^{52} - 1 = 141.04 = 14{,}104\%$$

That's not a misplaced comma above—we're talking over fourteen *thousand* percent. (Loan-sharking does have its benefits—if you can consistently collect the money, of course.)

CHAPTER 18
MUTUAL FUNDS

I.   SURVEYING THE TERRITORY: AN AERIAL VIEW

Mutual fund customers buy *shares* issued by the fund. The fund takes the proceeds and invests them in financial assets. On the surface, this isn't *light years* removed from what a bank does. But there is a difference. The buyer of mutual fund shares will be *participating directly* in the performance of the fund's investments. The customer has an equity-type claim. If the fund's investments do well, the customer does well. It's that simple.

And evidently, that simple idea is quite popular. In 1980, there were 564 mutual funds. By 2001, that number had ballooned to 8,307. (See text Table 18-1.) This growth was fueled by customer demands, of course. The number of mutual fund shareholders, over that same period, went from twelve-plus million to almost 248 million. Granted, there's a heavy dose of double counting in the customer figures—but there's no denying a major-league demand for mutual fund services.

By the way, why do we see so darned many funds? You might remember the *decrease* in the number of *depository* institutions we've observed, amidst all the bank consolidations. Well, compare a *bank account* with a *mutual fund share*. When we shop for a bank account… just how many different variations on the "deposit theme" can there be? We're basically looking at a *fixed-rate* account. But when we shop for a mutual fund… we can pick and choose from funds investing in bonds, those investing in equities, those that dabble in both… and on and on and on.   There's a lot of opportunity to mix assets in various ways—offering different mixtures to different segments of the marketplace. And let's admit it: perhaps there's more opportunity for the *marketing wizards* to apply their magic in the fund business.

The major topics of the chapter:

Mutual Funds: Chapter Overview

Size, Structure, and Composition of the Industry

Balance Sheet and Recent Trends

Regulation

Global Issues

Appendix: Hedge Funds
(accessible at: **www.mhhe.com/sc2e**)

II.   DIGGING IN THE DIRT: A SUBTERRANEAN VIEW

Key terms

equity funds
bond funds
hybrid funds
long-term funds
short-term funds
money market mutual funds (MMMFs)
tax exempt money market mutual fund
prospectus
aggressive growth
marked to market
net asset value (NAV)
open-end mutual fund
closed-end investment company
Morningstar
REIT
load fund
no-load fund
management fee
12b-1 fees
Securities and Exchange Act
NASD
Investment Advisors Act
Investment Company Act
National Securities Market Improvement Act

Got a question?

1. This is a short-term mutual fund, which invests in money market securities—those having original maturity of less than one year. This is the: _____.

2. The asset values of a mutual fund are typically _____ on a daily basis, meaning that the fund managers determine the market values of securities held by the fund each day.

3. The _____ of 1940 established rules to prevent conflicts of interest, fraud, and excessive fees or charges for fund shares.

4. This is one type of investment company. The supply of its shares outstanding is *not* fixed; investor demand for the shares basically determines how many will be sold. This is a/an: _____.

5. This is a type of mutual fund that does not charge an initial sales fee, or commission.
   This is a/an: _____.

6. The _____ of 1934 requires mutual funds to furnish full and accurate information on all financial and corporate matters to prospective fund purchasers.

7. One type of mutual fund is called an **asset allocation fund**. This type would be found in the broader category known as:
   _____.

8. Regulations require that mutual funds specify their investment objectives in a _____, which is made available to potential investors.

9. The _____ of 1996 exempts mutual fund sellers from oversight by state securities regulators, thereby reducing their regulatory burden.

10. _____ is a leading provider of data and performance measurement information on closed-end and open-end funds.

11. Take the market value of the assets in a fund's portfolio, and divide by the number of mutual fund shares outstanding. The result is known as the:
   _____.

12. So-called _____ are fees charged by mutual funds to cover costs of marketing and distribution of the fund's shares.

13. A _____ is an investment company having a *fixed* number of shares outstanding.

14. An _____ mutual fund is one that invests in securities of the highest-growth and highest-risk firms.

15. *Growth*, *Sector*, and *Aggressive Growth* funds: these are all fund types found within the larger fund category called: _____.

16. What are the three underlying aspects of the return, for an investor in a mutual fund?

17. How have mutual fund asset holdings compared with asset holdings of some other, major financial institutions in recent years?

18. What would be the argument for using a **load fund**, rather than a **no-load fund**? In terms of numbers of funds, which category seems to be winning out?

Got a problem?

1. A mutual fund owns three stocks; the amounts and prices are listed below:

Home Depot	10,000 shares	$56.00
Hewlett Packard	16,000	114.50
Kimberly Clark	8,000	58.00

    The mutual fund has 50,000 shares outstanding. What is the **net asset value** of a share?

2. Continuing with the mutual fund from the preceding problem, suppose investors buy 2,000 additional shares—at the NAV determined in the preceding problem. The fund uses the proceeds to purchase Home Depot stock (at the price indicated in the preceding problem).
    a) What is the value of the mutual fund's assets, immediately after it issues the new shares?
    b) How many shares of Home Depot does the fund purchase?
    c) A few days later, the following prices are observed for the three stocks held by the fund. Compute the new **net asset value** of the fund.

Home Depot	$ 50.00
Hewlett Packard	113.50
Kimberly Clark	58.00

3. John mailed in a check for $6,000 to White Cloud Fund. This mutual fund charges a 3% front-end load. Also, White Cloud has an expense ratio equal to 1% of the investor's average account value. One year after John's investment, it turns out that White Cloud's portfolio has earned 7.5%.
    a) What was John's account value immediately after investing?
    b) What was John's account value at the end of one year, but just before the management fee is paid?
    c) What was John's share of the annual expenses? (We're assuming the expense is computed after John has been in the fund for one year.) Also, what is John's account balance after the annual expense is deducted?
    d) What is John's rate of return for the year?

Web cruising ideas

1. The Investment Company Institute (ICI) is a great source for mutual fund industry data. In fact, it is the source for many of the statistics mentioned in the text. The entryway is:

    http://www.ici.org/

2. If you want to look up some specific mutual fund companies, the ICI site can help with that, too, by providing links. Go to:

    http://www.ici.org/newsroom/websites.html

3. An annual source of mutual fund statistics, also sponsored by ICI, is the *Mutual Fund Fact Book*. You can find it at:

    http://www.ici.org/facts_figures/factbook_toc.html

III. WASHING UP... AND THE "ABC" AWARDS

A. The EASIEST THING in the chapter

Look at text Table 18-7 on the twenty *largest* mutual funds. One striking thing: note how *easy* it's been to *lose* money! Every fund in the table turned in a *negative* 12-month return (as reported in July, 2002). And remember, these are *big, fat* mutual funds—successful funds, having attracted lots of investor interest.

Of course, not every 12-month period will look quite so bleak as what we see in Table 18-7. In fact, just a few short years ago, we would have observed *whopping big* returns for lots of mutual funds. Then, it looked incredibly *easy* to make money. In the early 2000s, the story changed dramatically.

B. The HARDEST THING in the chapter

It is still hard to understand how *so many* mutual funds could have sprung up over the years. True, the creative mind has no limits when it comes to new marketing strategies. But going from a few hundred to *thousands* of funds—over just a couple of decades—is still hard to fathom. Are we getting *less* risk averse? Or maybe, more knowledgeable about accepting calculated risks? Also...it's possible that the content of the *next* chapter—on pensions—has something to do with it.

C. The FUNNIEST THING in the chapter... or not

There are *so many* funds, it can be fun to browse around the web, looking for unique or unusual investment philosophies.

Want to find funds with a *social conscience*? You might want to check out the Calvert Group, online at: http://www.calvertgroup.com/index.html. These folks won't invest in just any company that shows prospects for profits. Instead, if you check out their site, you'll see various limitations they've imposed on themselves—for example, they search for companies that operate in an "environmentally sustaining manner."

Does a particular religious view drive your investment thinking? It does for some folks. Take a look at an organization called *The Timothy Plan*. It claims to avoid investing in companies with practices "contrary to Judeo-Christian principles."

Whatever your personal preferences may be, one thing's for sure: the market is rich enough to provide quite a lot of variety!

IV.   CHECKING THE ANSWERS...FOR SECTION II

Terms:
1. money market mutual funds (MMMFs)
2. marked to market
3. Investment Company Act
4. open-end mutual fund
5. no-load fund
6. Securities and Exchange Act
7. hybrid funds (which is also a "long-term" fund)
8. prospectus
9. National Securities Markets Improvement Act
10. Morningstar
11. net asset value (NAV)
12. 12b-1 fees
13. closed-end investment company
14. aggressive growth
15. equity funds

Essays:
16. First, the fund's portfolio may earn income, such as coupons and dividends received. Second, the fund may sell assets at appreciated prices. Third, appreciation of the fund assets (even if they are not sold) adds value to the mutual fund's share value.

17. Mutual funds have been doing quite well. Take a look at the text's Figure 18-1, which compares asset holdings, across institutional type, for 1990 and 2001. In 1990, mutual funds were behind commercial banks, private pension funds, insurance companies and state/local government pension funds. By 2001, mutual funds had moved way up—second only to commercial banks in asset size.

18. Advocates of using load funds argue that the investor will receive superior advice—the investors in such funds are often dealing with a broker. But the no load funds seem to be winning more battles in recent years. The text reports that in 1985, load funds accounted for 70 percent of all fund sales. By 1998, however, the sale of no-load funds exceeded that of load fund shares.

Problems:

1. First, multiply the shares by the stock price; then add.

    $$(\$56 \times 10{,}000) + (\$114.50 \times 16{,}000) + (\$58 \times 8{,}000) = \$2{,}856{,}000$$

    Now, divide the result by the number of *mutual fund* shares, to get the NAV.

    $$\$2{,}856{,}000 / 50{,}000 = \$57.12 = NAV$$

2. Remember that we start information from the preceding problem.
    a) The value just received by the fund, for the 2000 new shares, is

        $$2{,}000 \times \$57.12 = \$114{,}240$$

        Adding this to the previous value (\$2,856,000, determined above), we have \$2,970,240.

    b) With \$114,240 spent on Home Depot, at \$56 per share, the fund purchases 2,040 shares.

    c) Now, the funds assets are comprised of the following:

Home Depot	12,040 shares	\$50.00 price
Hewlett Packard	16,000	113.50
Kimberly Clark	8,000	58.00

        The fund's total asset value is:

        $$(\$50 \times 12{,}040) + (\$113.50 \times 16{,}000) + (\$58 \times 8{,}000) = \$2{,}882{,}000$$

        The fund's *net asset value:*

        $$NAV = \$2{,}882{,}000 \Big/ 52{,}000 = \$55.42$$

3. Two clues: first, this is a "load" fund, and second, the expense ratio will be applied to John's average account balance.
    a) The load is 3 percent of John's \$6,000 investment. That's \$180. John's account will have (1 - .03), or 97% of what he sent in: \$5,820.
    b) A rate of return of 7.5% means that John's account value will rise to (1.075) X \$5,820 = \$6,256.50. (Note: this is before any management fees are deducted.)

c) Applying the 1 percent management fee to John's average balance:

$$1\% \times \frac{\$5,820 + \$6,256.50}{2} = \$60.38$$

Now, deduct the fee to get John's year-end account balance:

$6,256.50 - $60.38 = $6,196.12

d) John's rate of return:

$$\frac{\$6,196.12 - \$6,000}{\$6,000} = .0338 = 3.38\%$$

Needless to say, the fees—and especially the load—make a big difference in John's actual return.

CHAPTER 19
PENSION FUNDS

I. SURVEYING THE TERRITORY: AN AERIAL VIEW

Pensions. One's interest in pensions just might be directly related to one's age. Come on, admit it... some readers surely know what I'm talking about. Suppose, at the ripe old age of 24, you're well into one of those extra-inning job interviews. You've already sold *them*. Now they're trying to sell *you*—with the human resources people telling you about perks, vacation... and the *pension plan*. Right after the vacation part, you may well take the hint, and mentally *go on vacation*. In contrast, if you're in that interview at the ripe old age of 44... well, at least you are probably able to keep your eyes open. But, at the ripe and musty old age of 54, ... heck, you're plugging in their numbers on the fly, doing "what-ifs" on your notebook computer! Advancing age has a way of focusing our attention, when the topic is pensions.

Pensions constitute a big part of the financial world... and a growing part too. Just note the *units of measurement* in the text's Table 19-1 or Figure 19-1. We're talking *trillions* of dollars. In terms of growth, take a look at the bottom line of Table 19-1, showing total pension fund reserves. From 1990 to 2001, the total reserves *more than doubled*. Why? Well, chalk it up to an advanced economy. For one thing, folks are living a lot longer. So the need for retirement income naturally becomes a bigger issue. And, from an employer's point of view, this is a compensation feature that may become more effective in an economy where the basics of life—like food and a roof, for the *here and now*—have already been covered.

Whatever the reason, pensions are big. They invest huge sums of money. Even if you're on the younger side of the age spectrum, a pension-related job could be in your future. Banks, insurance companies, mutual funds—they've seen the huge amount of assets devoted to pensions—and have been eager to get their share of it. Perhaps that can be motivation enough to pay attention to the topic.

The major topics of this chapter:

Pension Funds Defined: Chapter Overview

Size, Structure, and Composition of the Industry

Financial Asset Investments and Recent Trends

Regulation of Pension Funds

Global Issues

II.   DIGGING IN THE DIRT: A SUBTERRANEAN VIEW

Key terms

> **private pension fund**
> **public pension fund**
> **pension plan**
> **insured pension fund**
> **non-insured pension fund**
> **defined benefit pension plan**
> **flat benefit formula**
> **career average formula**
> **final pay formula**
> **fully funded**
> **underfunded**
> **overfunded**
> **defined contribution pension plan**
> **401(k) plan**
> **403(b) plan**
> **individual retirement account (IRA)**
> **Roth IRA**
> **traditional IRA**
> **Keogh account**
> **Old Age and Survivors Insurance Fund**
> **vested**
> **ERISA**
> **PBGC**

Got a question?

1. Another name for what we know as *Social Security* is:
   _____.

2. With a _____, the employee will receive a retirement benefit equal to some fixed amount, multiplied by the number of years of employment.

3. In a _____, the sponsor of the pension plan does *not* commit to the payment of specified pension benefits. Instead, it makes a specified contribution to the pension plan during the employee's working years.

4. A _____ is a pension plan administered by a federal, state, or local government.

5. If a pension plan is described as being _____, then the plan has sufficient funds available to meet all future payment obligations.

6. In 1998, the _____ account was established under the law. Contributions to these accounts are taxed in the year of contribution, while withdrawals are tax free (subject to certain restrictions).

7. This is a type of pension benefit scheme in which the payment is based on a percentage of the worker's average salary near career-end, multiplied by the number of years employed.
   This is the: _____.

8. A _____ is an employer-sponsored plan that supplements a firm's basic retirement plan, allowing for both employee and employer contributions. Employees generally have some discretion over how the funds are allocated among various kinds of assets.

9. A/an _____ is a retirement account available to self-employed individuals. Contributions by the individuals placed with a financial institution, and the participant generally has some discretion on how the funds are allocated.

10. A/an _____ is a self-directed retirement account set up by a individual who may also be covered by an employer-sponsored pension plan. Contributions are made only by the employee. A maximum of $2,000 may be contributed per year.

11. The insurance fund for pension plan participants, established in 1974, is known as: _____.

12. A _____ is a supplemental retirement plan, sponsored by certain tax exempt employers, such as hospitals and educational institutions.

13. When a person has worked for a firm long enough to be eligible for receiving pension benefits, we say that the person is: _____.

14. With a _____, a financial institution *other than a life insurance company* is appointed by the sponsoring business or union to administer the pension plan. Assets in such funds are owned by the sponsor.

15. Contrast **insured pension plans** and **noninsured pension plans**, in terms of the ownership and control of the *assets* that will be used to cover the payments to pension recipients.

16. In the area of private pension funds, how have *defined benefit plans* and *defined contribution plans* compared in recent history—in terms of numbers of plans, employees covered, and asset acquisitions? What accounts for these numbers?

17. Briefly, distinguish the tax-related features of a **Roth IRA** from those of a **traditional IRA**.

18. How does the issue of pension plan *funding* (e.g., fully funded or not) relate to *defined benefit plans* and *defined contribution plans*?

Got a problem?

1. Joe plans to contribute $3,000 per year to a Roth IRA. Joe is 25 years from retirement. How much will he will have accumulated upon retirement, given two alternative investment scenarios:
   a) Joe puts his IRA funds in an equity mutual fund, having a long-term expected annual return of 9%.
   b) Joe puts the funds in a less risky bond-oriented fund, having a long-term expected annual return of 5%.

For **problems 2-4**, consider the salary data of Emily:

Total years of service, upon retirement   33 years
Average salary, over entire employment $25,650
Annual salary, year by year, over *last three* years before retirement:
                              Year 31 $41,200
                              Year 32   43,800
                              Year 33   45,500

2. Suppose the pension plan uses a flat benefit formula, paying $1,000 per year of service. Compute Emily's annual pension benefit.

3. Suppose the pension plan uses a career average formula. The annual payout is 3.8% of career average salary, times the total years employed. Compute Emily's annual pension benefit.

4. Suppose the pension plan uses a final pay formula. The annual payout is 2.3% of the average salary of the last three years, times the total years employed. Compute Emily's annual pension benefit.

<u>Web cruising ideas</u>

1. The Pension Benefit Guarantee Corporation has an extensive web site. Here is the entryway:

   http://www.pbgc.gov/

2. One particular thing to look for at the PBGC's site is the premium structure. Go to the address above, and snoop around for *plan administration* information.

3. Know someone who *thought* they had a company pension coming, but it seemed to disappear? You might want to direct them to the *participant* part of the PBGC site, and tell them to look for "finding a lost pension."

III. WASHING UP... AND THE "ABC" AWARDS

A. The EASIEST THING in the chapter

Understanding the concept of a pension plan does not require new or fancy techniques. Frankly, it boils down to a basic application of present value/future value techniques. How much do we set aside *now*, in order to reach some targeted amount in the *future*? And we've already got that set of techniques in our toolkit.

B. The HARDEST THING in the chapter

One thing about pensions can be easy to overlook. It's an issue that arises when I put *someone else* in charge of something being done for *my* benefit. If I'm in a defined benefit pension plan, someone else is supposed to be worrying about how to invest the funds. But the "someone else" just might worry more about his or her own interests, perhaps taking on a bit more risk—at my expense. Of course, this is where ERISA comes in, setting standards for pension fund management. Pension plan assets are to be invested with the same care as we would expect from a "prudent person." But, will there always be a clear idea about what that mythical prudent person *should* do?

C. The FUNNIEST THING in the chapter... or not

In snooping around, trying my best to uncover something slightly hilarious about pensions, I was struck by how often I encountered web sites devoted to lists of pensioners...long-dead pensioners—from the Civil War, and yes, even the Revolutionary War. Why all this interest about pensions paid to people who are no longer around? Within a few seconds, it hit me: the *genealogists* among us have a great interest in those pensioner records. Have you been searching for missing branches in your family tree? Then maybe you've just become interested in military pension records. (You're right, this isn't even a *tiny bit* hilarious.)

IV. CHECKING THE ANSWERS... FOR SECTION II

Terms:

1. Old Age and Survivors Insurance Fund
2. flat benefit formula
3. defined contribution pension plan
4. public pension fund
5. fully funded (also, an overfunded plan would also meet the criterion here)
6. Roth IRA
7. final pay formula
8. 401(k) plan
9. Keogh account
10. individual retirement account (IRA)—and note that the Roth and traditional IRAs are sub-categories
11. PBGC (for Pension Benefit Guarantee Corporation)
12. 403(b) plan
13. vested
14. non-insured pension fund

Essays:

15. In a *noninsured plan*, the assets are owned by the plan sponsor (e.g., the business that employs the eventual pension recipient). A trust department would be appointed by the sponsor, to handle the investments and pay out the retirement benefits. In contrast, with an *insured plan*, a life insurance company has been chosen to administer the plan. It receives the premiums and invests them, and is the legal owner of the assets purchased. The insurance company then has a liability to cover the specified retirement benefits. The sponsoring organization does not own the assets that will be used to cover retirement benefits.

16. Defined contribution plans are increasingly dominating the market. The text's Table 19-3 shows that defined contribution plans have acquired significantly more assets in recent years, when compared with defined benefit plans. In terms of sheer numbers, the defined contribution plans far outnumber the defined benefit plans (see Figure 19-2). There are also more active participants in defined contribution plans (see Figure 19-3). With a defined contribution plan, the sponsoring employer is not guaranteeing benefits. As a result, the sponsor does not have the job of monitoring performance, to make sure than some specified set of promised benefits can be met in the future (there is no such promise).

17. With a traditional IRA, the annual contribution to the account can be fully deductible from taxable income (although there are important conditions on this). Later, when the individual withdraws funds during retirement, income taxes are paid on the contributions and earnings. In contrast, with a Roth IRA, the contributions are not tax deductible. When the eventual withdrawals are made, no

taxes are paid. (Note that we're making a very general comparison—the law contains many details, not described here.)

18. The issue of funding only arises in the context of a *defined benefit plan*. This type of plan has promised (i.e., "defined") as schedule of benefits for the employees. There is a problem to grapple with: having sufficient funds available for payout when they are needed. By contrast, in a *defined contribution plan*, no benefits have been scheduled. Instead, only the *contributions* are scheduled (i.e., "defined"). With this type of plan, the employee simply receives a benefit based on "what's available," given the size of the contributions and the investment performance.

Problems:

1. These are basic future value problems—specifically, for an annuity. Of course, the assumed annual return is very crucial to the outcome.

   a) $FV = FVIFA_{9\%,25} \times \$3,000 = 84.7009 \times \$3,000 = \$254,102.69$

   b) $FV = FVIFA_{6\%,25} \times \$3,000 = 54.8654 \times \$3,000 = \$164,593.54$

   If you're using a financial calculator, the $3,000 goes in your PMT register, and you're solving for FV. We're assuming that Joe contributes his funds at the end of each year.

2. Pretty simple: years of service (33) times $1,000, or $33,000.

3. A bit more complicated: The magical percentage (3.8%) times the lifetime average salary ($25,650) times years of service (33). Result: $32,165.10.

4. Similar to problem 2, but now, the last three years are of prime importance: The magical percentage (2.3%) times last three years' average salary ($43,500) times years of service (33). Result: $33,016.50.

CHAPTER 20
TYPES OF RISK INCURRED BY FINANCIAL INSTITUTIONS

I. SURVEYING THE TERRITORY: AN AERIAL VIEW

Risk is at the heart of finance. And while we have already encountered it earlier in the text, you might say we are now arriving at *Close Encounters of the Risk Kind*. Chapter 20 provides an overview of some issues taken up in subsequent chapters.

Credit risk, interest rate risk, sovereign risk, market risk,... and on and on. In a sense, Chapter 20 is a sort of *library*, where risks are neatly categorized. That's just one metaphor, of course. The task here is similar to that of a biologist. In the biology lab, the animals and plants get sliced up and examined. Comparisons are made. Distinctive characteristics are noted. Likewise, we're trying to examine various "risk animals," making distinctions among them.

But a reminder is in order. In your *real world* encounters with risk—let's say in a financial institution, where you are managing financial assets and dealing with clients—the various risks might not seem so distinct. Back in the biology lab, we can put a specimen under the microscope and examine it closely, in isolation. But when we step out of the lab and go into the field, we face a more difficult task. Now, the animals are in their natural habitat. They may blend in with their surroundings, and it can be hard to see them at all, let alone make important distinctions among them. And so it is with credit risk, interest rate risk... and all the others. These risks may *all* be there at the same time. They won't come up and introduce themselves, by name!

Perhaps we've just touched upon the biggest risk of all—knowing just what classes of uncertainties we're up against, in a given real-world situation.

The main topics of the chapter:

Why Financial Institutions Need to Manage Risk: Chapter Overview

Credit Risk

Liquidity Risk

Interest Rate Risk

Market Risk

Off-Balance-Sheet Risk

Foreign Exchange Risk

Country or Sovereign Risk

Technology and Operational Risk

Insolvency Risk

Other Risks and Interaction among Risks

II.   **DIGGING IN THE DIRT: A SUBTERRANEAN VIEW**

Key terms

>   **credit risk**
>   **firm-specific credit risk**
>   **systematic credit risk**
>   **liquidity risk**
>   **interest rate risk**
>   **market risk**
>   **off-balance-sheet risk**
>   **letter of credit**
>   **foreign exchange risk**
>   **country or sovereign risk**
>   **technology risk**
>   **operational risk**
>   **insolvency risk**

Got a question?

1. The risk that exchange rates change, thereby changing the values of a financial institution's assets and liabilities denominated in foreign currencies is called: _____.

2. The risk of default due to factors that simultaneously increase the default risk of all firms in the economy is called: _____.

3. A _____ is a guarantee issued by a financial institution, for a fee. The guarantee's payoff is contingent on some future event— most likely the default of the purchaser of the guarantee.

4. Bank of Mudville's assets have suffered a decline in value, and it is sufficiently large that the value may be less than the bank's asset value. This shows an example of: _____.

5. _____ is simply the risk that the promised cash flows from loans and securities held by financial institutions may not be paid in full.

6. _____ _____ arises when technology or back-office support systems are subject to breakdown.

7. One type of risk is that technological investments do not produce the anticipated cost savings.
   This is called: _____.

8. This is a type of credit risk that is not due to economy-wide factors. Hence, diversification by the financial institution can reduce its exposure to such risks.
   This is called: _____.

9. If a financial institution's liability holders—such as depositors at a bank—may demand cash immediately, the institution is subject to the risk of being able to meet those demands.
   This risk is called: _____.

10. One class of activities does not affect the assets or liabilities on the institution's balance sheet *now*. Instead, they involve they involve the potential for assets or liabilities to appear in the future.
    The risk of engaging in such activities is called: _____.

11. If a financial institution's assets and liabilities have different maturities, the institution is likely exposed to a type of risk called:
    _____.

12. This is a risk faced by institutions that actively trade assets and liabilities; in fact, it could also be termed "trading risk." It is closely related to interest rate risk and foreign exchange risk.
    This is: _____.

13. An American institution buys fixed-rate, coupon-paying bonds issued by a German firm. The bonds are denominated in marks. Describe the various risks associated with such a purchase.

14. An institution may face "refinancing risk" which is very much like "reinvestment risk." Further, both of these can be viewed as examples of one of the major kinds of risk mentioned in the chapter. Explain.

15. BankTwenty has earning assets of $1.5 billion. It is earning a fixed rate of 12% on them. The assets mature in two years. BankTwenty also has interest-bearing liabilities of $1.5 billion. The interest rate on the liabilities floats with the market; currently the rate is 6%. *Explain* the nature of the risk faced by BankTwenty. (Don't worry about calculations at this point—just answer the question *qualitatively*.)

16. U.S. Global Corp. raises $160 million in the U.S. It is paying 8% annually on the funds. It converts the dollars to British pounds (current exchange rate: $1.60 per pound), and invests the funds in England, earning a rate of 11%. The maturities of the investments and liabilities are the same.
    a) Explain the nature of the risk faced by U.S. Global in this transaction.
    b) What additional risk would result if maturities were *not* matched?

Got a problem?

1. Refer to the information given in essay question **15**—on **BankTwenty**.
   a) Suppose market interest rates do not change over the coming two years. Compute BankTwenty's annual net interest income over the next two years. (For simplicity, assume interest is paid just once per year, and don't worry about compounding.)
   b) Suppose that market interest rates do not change for one year, but then *rise* by *one percentage point*. Compute the bank's annual net interest income over the next two years.
   c) Suppose that market interest rates do not change for one year, but then *fall* by *one percentage point*. Compute the bank's annual net interest income over the next two years.

2. Refer to the information given in essay question **16**—on **U.S. Global Corp.** Also, for simplicity, you can assume that interest is paid (and received) just once per year.
   a) If the exchange rate remains unchanged, what is U.S. Global's annual net interest income (in U.S. dollars) from the transaction?
   b) If the exchange rate changes to $1.70 per pound at the end of one year, determine the company's annual net interest income, in dollars.
   c) If the exchange rate changes to $1.50 per pound at the end of one year, determine the company's annual net interest income, in dollars.

Web cruising ideas

We'll take a brief vacation from cruising here...although, not entirely. Take a look at our latest, feeble attempt at humor—coming up on the next page.

III. WASHING UP... AND THE "ABC" AWARDS

A. The EASIEST THING in the chapter

It's easy to *talk about* the weather. But, *doing something* about it—well, that's another matter. And so it is with *risk*. Chapter 20 *talks about it*, but we aren't asked to *do anything* about it.

B. The HARDEST THING in the chapter

The hardest thing might be getting a good feel for what the text called the "interaction" among different risks. It does make sense to divide up problems and deal with the parts separately, one at a time—and that's what we've done with the problem of risk. But dealing effectively with *one* particular risk doesn't mean we have dealt with *all* risks effectively.

C. The FUNNIEST THING in the chapter... or not

Like many readers, I was under the impression that Chapter 20 provided a thorough, wide-ranging overview of the different kinds of risk. Just to check that premise, I did a quick and dirty World Wide Web search—based on one key word: RISK. Guess which of our specific risk categories seemed most popular, in terms of web links? ...Well, how about *none of the above*? Now, this was a strictly informal search; no particular threshold of statistical significance is being claimed. What exactly did I encounter? There were a *whole bunch* of references to food and disease risks. In fact, lots of the links took me to the U.S. Food and Drug Administration's "Bad Bug Book"—you know, the bugs that can make us sick. (Guess we'll have to add *bad bug risks* to the text's Table 20-1.)

IV.   CHECKING THE ANSWERS... FOR SECTION II

Terms:
1. foreign exchange risk
2. systematic credit risk
3. letter of credit
4. insolvency risk
5. credit risk
6. operational risk
7. technology risk
8. firm-specific credit risk
9. liquidity risk
10. off-balance-sheet risk
11. interest rate risk
12. market risk

Essays:
13. First, there is *credit risk*, since the issuer could default on the payments. Second, there is *interest rate risk*, due to two things: (a) reinvestment of coupon payments at the (unknown) future interest rates, and (b) possible "mismatching" of this security relative to obligations of the purchasing institution. Third, there is *foreign exchange risk*, because the dollar value of the mark may change. Theoretically, there could also be *sovereign risk*, meaning that there could be interference in the bond's payment from the German government (although there is nothing in the question's premise to suggest this particular problem.)

14. *Reinvestment risk* occurs when cash flows are received from an investment: the cash inflows must be redeployed, in new investments. Examples would be periodic receipts of interest or principal payments, as on a loan or a bond. The risk is due to the uncertainty in *interest rates*, which affects the return on the *reinvested* cash flows. Likewise, *refinancing risk* occurs when new financing must be arranged—for example, when a short-term deposit comes due and the bank must come up with new funding to replace it. Just as in the case of reinvestment risk, refinancing risk is due to a more general class of risk—interest rate risk. Refinancing risk is just like reinvestment risk, but it is rooted on the opposite side of the balance sheet—the liability side.

15. BankTwenty faces an *interest rate risk* problem. And, its particular problem is a classic one: it has *borrowed short*, while *lending long*. It's liabilities, in other words, have a shorter maturity than its assets. If market interest rates should *rise*, BankTwenty will be paying more interest on its liabilities, while its assets still earn their fixed rate of 12%. Net interest income will decline. With risk comes opportunity, however: if market rates should *fall*, the cost of the floating rate liabilities will fall, while the revenue generated by the fixed rate assets will stay the same. Net interest income will rise. One final thing: there could be *other*

risks, too. While the question does not suggest other, particular kinds of risk, the earning assets might well be subject to credit risk.

16. U.S. Global:
    a) The firm faces the risk of exchange rate changes. It owes U.S. dollars to its liability holders. But it has invested in assets denominated in pounds. It will receive 11% on its English investment, paid in *pounds*. When U.S. Global receives the interest, the pound may be *stronger* or *weaker* than it was when the transaction was initiated—and this will affect U.S. Global's profitability. If the pound should be worth *more* than $1.60, for example, then the pounds will convert to *more* dollars, and U.S. Global will benefit.
    b) Since the maturities are equal, the *interest rate risk* is likely to be minimal. On the asset and liability side of U.S. Global's balance sheet, interest rates are fixed for the same length of time. But if maturities are *not* matched, interest rate risk can become an additional problem. (Note: Here, we see reference to *maturity*, but no mention of *duration*. This is primarily for the sake of simplicity. Maturity would be a reasonable indicator of risk, if we are concerned mainly with changes in net interest income. If we are more concerned with changing *values* of assets and liabilities, *duration* would be a desirable risk yardstick.)

Problems:
1. For BankTwenty:
   a) Subtract the interest expense from the interest income:

   $$(12\% \times \$1.5) - (6\% \times \$1.5) = \$.09 \text{ billion}$$

   This would be the net interest income in *each* of the coming two years—assuming interest rates do not change, and assuming no new assets and liabilities.

   b) First, the net interest income for the *first year* is the same as indicated in part (a). At the end of one year, rates *rise* by one percentage point, so the rate paid on liabilities goes from 6% to 7%. Note that the rate on the assets remains fixed, at 12%. So, in the *second year*, we have:

   $$(12\% \times \$1.5) - (7\% \times \$1.5) = \$.075 \text{ billion}$$

   Net interest income falls in the second year.

   c) Again, the *first year* shows no change from part (a). If rates *fall* by one percentage point, the *second year* net interest income rises:

   $$(12\% \times \$1.5) - (5\% \times \$1.5) = \$.105 \text{ billion}$$

2. For U.S. Global:

a) It has invested $160 million, or 100 million pounds (at $1.60 per pound). It is earning 11% on these assets, or 11 million pounds. Converting this back to dollars, we have earnings of $17.6 million. It pays 8% on the $160 million it raised in the U.S., or $12.8 million. Its net interest income is: $17.6 - $12.8 or $4.8 million.

b) The 100 million in pounds has still earned 11 million pounds, just as in part (a). But with a *stronger pound*, the conversion to dollars is:

$$\$1.70 \times \$11 = \$18.7 \text{ million}$$

The net interest income is now: $18.7 - $12.8, or $5.9 million

c) The only thing changing is the conversion of the pound income into dollars, or:

$$\$1.50 \times \$11 = \$16.5 \text{ million}$$

Net interest income: $16.5 - $12.8, or $3.7 million

CHAPTER 21
MANAGING RISK ON THE BALANCE SHEET I:
CREDIT RISK

I. SURVEYING THE TERRITORY: AN AERIAL VIEW

Credit risk is probably the most obvious risk. A bank typically derives most of its revenue from lending. But there is always a chance that the borrower will not repay. It's pretty much the same basic situation with a bond. A company, or a government, has sold a security, promising to pay the money back, with interest. But they *might not pay*—or might not pay *on time*. Our problem is how to *assess* such risk.

At a very general level, assessing credit risk requires a look at data from the borrower's past—what "tracks" have been left in the sand, from other financial transactions? Are there lots of debts on the balance sheet? Has the borrower been paying existing debts as promised? How will the required loan payments stack up against the borrower's expected cash flow? What about the cash flow—has it been growing, and does it seem secure? And, if operational cash flow should take a dive, can the collateral provide adequate backup?

At a more specific level, credit analysts apply a set of quantitative tools—which then are used to make judgments about the borrower's credit worthiness. The starting point is data on a loan application, or possibly on a set of financial statements (for a business borrower). Financial ratios are computed, and comparisons are made. Some analysts have taken the ratio analysis a step further, by trying to link various ratios, statistically, to the probability of default. This is *credit scoring*. In essence, credit scoring is an attempt to systematize credit analysis, substituting an objective model for case-by-case human judgments. A classic example of this approach, applied to business default risk, is Altman's Z-Score.

Note one crucial thing about the whole process: credit is extended *now*, but it will be repaid from funds available in the *future*. In credit analysis, we're hoping to use those "tracks in the sand" to tell us about the *future*. And, in the world of finance, we are often humbled by our meager abilities to predict what tomorrow will bring.

Credit Risk Management: Chapter Overview

Credit Analysis

Calculating the Return on a Loan

Appendix: Loan Portfolio Risk and Management
(appendix accessible at **www.mhhe.com/sc2e**)

II.   DIGGING IN THE DIRT: A SUBTERRANEAN VIEW

Key terms

- junk bond
- nonperforming loans
- GDS (gross debt service) ratio
- TDS (total debt service) ratio
- credit scoring system
- perfecting
- foreclosure
- power of sale
- five Cs of credit
- liquidity ratios
- asset management ratios
- debt and solvency ratios
- profitability ratios
- EBIT
- EAT
- common size analysis
- conditions precedent
- Altman's Z-Score
- KMV Model
- RAROC
- ROA
- LIBOR
- prime lending rate
- origination fee
- compensating balance

Got a question?

1. _____ is a short-hand expression for an important income statement item, *earnings before interest and taxes*.

2. A _____ is the *general* term for the use of a quantitative model that uses observed characteristics of a loan applicant to calculate a "score," related to the applicant's probability of default.

3. When a lending institution goes though a process of ensuring that collateral is "free and clear" to the lender, if the borrower should default, we say that the lending institution is _____ the collateral.

4. This is a specific model designed to assess the credit risk of publicly traded manufacturing firms. It employs company financial ratios to categorize firms into two categories: no default and default.
    This is: _____.

5. The *current ratio* and *quick ratio* are both examples of a major class of financial ratios known as: _____.

6. Traditionally, the _____ was the rate charged to the bank's lowest risk customers. Now, it is more like a *base* rate, to which positive or negative premiums are added.

7. Character, capacity, capital, collateral, and conditions: These represent things relevant to a potential borrowing situation—which should be assessed before a loan is approved. Collectively, these things are known as the: _____.

8. A _____ is a bond rated as speculative or less than investment grade by bond-rating agencies, such as Moody's.

9. The model known as _____ views the equity value of a firm as equivalent to a call option on the assets of the firm. Given the amount of debt outstanding, the probability of a default by the firm can be calculated.

10. This is a measurement of a customer's ability to maintain mortgage payments. It is calculated by dividing the total annual accommodation expenses (annual mortgage payments and property taxes) by the borrowers' annual gross income. This is the: _____.

11. A _____ is the process of taking possession of the mortgaged property in satisfaction of a defaulting borrower's debt obligation.

12. Gross margin, return on equity, return on assets, income to sales: These ratios would all be categorized as: _____.

13. Large banks in the United States and Europe have adopted the _____ model. This measurement calls for expected annual loan income to be divided by value (or capital) at risk on the loan.

14. The *number of days sales in receivables* and the *sales to working capital* ratios are both examples of a major class of financial ratios called: _____.

15. When a credit analyst divides all the balance sheet items by *total assets*, and all income statement items by *total sales or revenue*, the analyst is conducting a: _____.

16. When using financial ratios to assess a borrower, what are the general types of comparison made by the financial institution?

17. What are the basic parts of a cash flow statement? When analyzing a typical business loan, which part of the cash flow may be most important?

18. What is Altman's Z-Score designed to accomplish? Under what circumstances would you be willing to use Altman's Z-Score—if at all?

Got a problem?

1. Joan is applying for a mortgage loan. The following information has been gathered in Joan's loan application process:

Gross monthly income:	$3,800
Existing auto loan pmt/month:	430
Existing finance company pmt./month:	105
Proposed mortgage pmt./month:	665
Annual property taxes on proposed home:	2,400

   a) Compute Joan's GDS (gross debt service).
   b) Compute Joan's TDS (total debt service).
   c) How would these measurements be interpreted?

2. Suppose the following represents information from a publicly traded manufacturing firm. Compute *Altman's Z-Score*. Interpret the result.

Total assets	$ 250 million
Current assets	95
Current liabilities	70
Long-term debt (book)	100
Total equity (book)	80
Retained earnings	55
EBIT	13
Sales	270
Market value of equity	90

3. New State Bank's current base lending rate is 8%. It faces a 10 percent required reserve ratio on demand deposits, imposed by the Federal Reserve. New State is considering a business loan applicant. The bank's credit analysis suggests that the borrower's risk is consistent with a 2 percent risk premium. If New State charges a quarter of a percent origination fee on the loan amount, and requires the borrower to maintain a 5% compensating balance in its checking account, compute the bank's **return on assets** for this customer.

Web cruising ideas

1.   Bank regulators have a wealth of banking information, with a lot of it available on their web sites. One particular page, of particular interest for the topic of *credit risk*, is the FDIC's semiannual report on underwriting practices at banks. The report is derived from information taken by FDIC bank examiners. You can find it at:

   http://www.fdic.gov/bank/analytical/report/index.html

   A couple of things you can look for:

   a) Check out the *objectives* established for this particular report.
   b) Also, bring up a recent report, and take a look at the assessment of current underwriting trends.

2. One firm involved in quantitative credit assessment is KMV (which recently became part of another well-known credit market institution—Moody's). It can be useful to see their own description of what they do. But remember, they won't want to *give* you everything they do for clients—after all, they're in business to *sell* their services. Here is their address:

   http://www.moodyskmv.com/

III.   WASHING UP... AND THE "ABC" AWARDS

A.   The EASIEST THING in the chapter

The easiest thing is appreciating the importance of the chapter's topic, credit risk. Frankly, when folks think about risk in a financial institution, *credit risk* is the first thing that comes to mind.

B.   The HARDEST THING in the chapter

It is hard to appreciate the analysis of credit risk *in the abstract*. Sure, we can try our hands at financial ratio analysis, cash flow projections, computing a Z-Score, and so on. And, with practice, we can get the *analytics* down. But understanding those analytics isn't quite the same as *taking a stand*, based on the numbers—i.e., answering the bottom-line question: *should we make that loan, or not?*

C.   The FUNNIEST THING in the chapter... or not

I've never cared much for watching golf on TV. With apologies to golf enthusiasts in the audience, watching an iceberg melt might be more interesting to me. But a serious, TV-watching golf fan gave me a very good, *logical* reason for why *he* watches: *"It feels good when I see that even the pros can hit some really lousy shots."*

Just where are we going here...?

Well.... what might constitute a *bad shot,* in the lending game? Take a look at the text's **In the News, 21-1.** The gist of the story is that WorldCom Inc. borrowed multi-millions, from a group of well-known banks. Later, WorldCom revealed some accounting discrepancies—basically meaning that profits weren't what the bankers (and other investors) had been led to believe. Those well-known banks—including the likes of Mellon, J.P. Morgan, Citigroup, and Fleet Boston—found their credits in serious doubt. The prospect of loan losses led banking analysts to lower their projections of the banks' earnings.

Bottom line: Even the "big and famous" players are *not invincible.* They are perfectly capable of a bad shot—maybe even a *really lousy shot.*

IV. CHECKING THE ANSWERS… FOR SECTION II

Terms:
1. EBIT
2. credit scoring system (Altman's Z-Score is a *specific* example)
3. perfecting
4. Altman's Z-Score
5. liquidity ratios
6. prime lending rate
7. five Cs of credit
8. junk bond
9. KMV model
10. GDS (gross debt service) ratio
11. foreclosure
12. profitability ratios
13. RAROC
14. asset management ratios
15. common size analysis

Essays:
16. There are two standard types of comparison: (1) comparison of the ratios with an appropriate peer group, and (2) comparison of the ratios with the firm's own historical ratios. The basic objective is to look for deviations, or "red flags," that might signal a need for a more detailed analysis. Also, some financial institutions may have "threshold" levels for certain ratios, which they will use in their comparisons.

17. There are three basic sources of cash flow: operations, financing activities, and investing activities. "Operations" includes the defining activities of the business: the revenues generated from selling the product or service, and the costs incurred in producing and selling the output. In general, cash flow from operations would be viewed as the most important cash flow when conducting a credit analysis. If the basic operations of the business have insufficient capacity to service a loan, the viability of the loan is doubtful.

18. Altman took a sample of publicly traded manufacturing companies, and tried to use a few financial ratios to *statistically explain* the occurrence of bankruptcy. In other words, he already knew what had happened to firms in his sample— bankruptcy or no bankruptcy—but here's the question he attacked: could he use a mixture of financial ratios to categorize, or "predict," where firms would end up? The mixture of financial ratios is captured by the Z-Score equation in the text. We wouldn't want to apply the equation to any and all circumstances. Different kinds of firms, at different times, might not be well "explained" by the Altman model. Also, while the information captured by the ratios is, for the most part, familiar data from company financial statements, there is one important exception: *market value of equity/book value of long-term debt*. The numerator is

not from the financial statements, but instead, comes from the market's valuation of the company's stock. This reminds us of the danger of trying to apply the equation to firms that are *not* publicly traded.

Problems:
1. Note that both the GDS ratio and the TDS ratio call for *annual* numbers.
   a) For the GDS, it's the proposed mortgage payments that matter:

$$GDS = \frac{(\$665 \times 12) + \$2,400}{\$3,800 \times 12} = .228 = 22.8\%$$

   b) For the TDS, we take all of Joan's debt payments:

$$TDS = \frac{(\$665 \times 12) + \$2,400 + (\$430 \times 12) + (\$105 \times 12)}{\$3,800 \times 12} = .368 = 36.8\%$$

   c) The text mentions threshold levels of: 25-30 percent for the GDS ratio, and 35-40 percent for the TDS ratio. Joan's TDS level suggests she would probably pass the test in terms of her overall debts. But her GDS ratio looks a bit on the low side. Note, however, that different institutions can set their own specific thresholds. Beyond that, however, note that these ratios provide only a "quick and dirty" method for screening applicants. In all likelihood, Joan might be an applicant whose ratios suggest closer scrutiny. The lender may look more closely at Joan's job situation (for evidence of job security and possible income growth) and the maturities of her existing debts.

2. Altman's Z-Score is calculated as:

$$Z = 1.2X_1 + 1.4X_2 + 3.3X_3 + 0.6X_4 + 1.0X_5$$

   where X_1 = working capital/total assets
   $\qquad X_2$ = retained earnings/total assets
   $\qquad X_3$ = earnings before interest and taxes/total assets
   $\qquad X_4$ = market value of equity/book value of long-term debt
   $\qquad X_5$ = sales/total assets

   Here, you have to compute a few ratios before plugging into the above equation.

$$X_1 = \frac{\$95 - \$70}{\$250} = .10$$

$$X_2 = \frac{\$55}{\$250} = .22$$

$$X_3 = \frac{\$13}{\$250} = .052$$

$$X_4 = \frac{\$90}{\$100} = .90$$

$$X_5 = \frac{\$270}{\$250} = 1.08$$

Plugging into the equation for Z:

$$Z = (1.2 \times .10) + (1.4 \times .22) + (3.3 \times .052) + (0.6 \times .90) + (1.0 \times 1.08) = 2.22$$

As mentioned in the text, a firm with a Z-Score less than 1.81 is to be interpreted as a high default risk firm. Consequently, this particular firm seems to "look good." Note, however, that Altman's equation was determined from a sampling of firms many years ago. Application of such an equation to current-day firms might take us into dangerous waters.

3. We can use the text's example 21-5 as a guide here. In the expression below, k is the return on assets:

$$1 + k = 1 + \frac{.0025 + (.08 + .02)}{1 - [.05(1 - .10)]} = 1 + .1073$$

So the return on assets is .1073, or 10.73%.

CHAPTER 22
MANAGING RISK ON THE BALANCE SHEET II:
LIQUIDITY RISK

I.   SURVEYING THE TERRITORY: AN AERIAL VIEW

So, how much have you got in *cash*?

Got some stocks, too? Okay, what can you *get* for them—*today*?

A house? Well, what's it worth if you sell it—*today*?

What's with the nosey questions? It's all about our theme: *liquidity*. The issue is how much *cash* you can put your mitts on… and in a *hurry*.

How can we measure liquidity? Adding up the cash is easy enough. But, what about other assets? A lot depends on whether the market for the asset is wide and deep… or thin and shallow. A big-time real estate investor could be quite wealthy, yet *illiquid*. To turn real estate into cash, we've got to search for a buyer. That may take time. Are there lots of potential purchasers? Or is this pile of bricks designed for a very special purpose? Of course, we could hurry up the process by offering them at a "fire sale" price. But that's the essence of an *illiquid* asset—it takes *time,* and probably a monetary inducement, to turn the asset into cash.

Financial institutions are facing exactly the same problem. They invest in loans and other securities. Some of these assets cannot be turned into cash very quickly. But the bank has to be ready when a depositor makes a big withdrawal. Likewise, an insurance company may have to write checks to the victims of yesterday's tornado. One issue addressed in Chapter 22 is how to measure an institution's liquidity. But beyond that, how can institutions respond to the challenge of having *sufficient* liquidity? Basically, they can do two kinds of things: (1) hold more "cash-like" assets, or (2) be ready to borrow cash in a hurry.

The major topics of the chapter:

Liquidity Risk Management: Chapter Overview

Causes of Liquidity Risk

Liquidity Risk and Depository Institutions

Liquidity Risk and Insurance Companies

Liquidity Risk and Mutual Funds

II.   DIGGING IN THE DIRT: A SUBTERRANEAN VIEW

Key terms

> fire-sale price
> liability side liquidity risk
> core deposits
> net deposit drain
> purchased liquidity
> stored liquidity
> asset side liquidity risk
> BIS maturity ladder analysis
> liquidity index
> financing gap
> financing requirement
> bank run
> bank panic
> deposit insurance
> discount window
> surrender value

Got a question?

1. When a depository institution experiences a sudden and unexpected jump in deposit withdrawals, we say the institution is experiencing a: _____.

2. The amount an insurance policyholder receives when cashing in a policy early is called: _____.

3. A bank's _____ provides a measurement of liquidity risk, and is computed by subtracting average core deposits from average loans.

4. Banks can meet short-term liquidity needs by borrowing at the Federal Reserve's _____.

5. Suppose a bank responds to a drain on deposits by entering the money markets to acquire short-term funds, such as federal funds. This bank is relying on _____ as it method of acquiring liquidity.

6. The term _____ refers to a relatively stable, long-term funding source for a bank. Among other things, it would typically include most of the bank's demand deposits.

7. Implementing the _____ requires a bank to measure anticipated cash inflows and cash outflows over a series of future time intervals. The objective is to assess the bank's future funding requirements.

8. When a bank run takes on contagious proportions, with depositors withdrawing funds from the banking industry as a whole, we describe the problem as a: _____.

9. Uncertainty about the volume of loan requests—for example, not knowing exactly when a bank customer might exercise of a loan commitment—is the basic cause of: _____.

10. When a depository institution is confronted with deposit withdrawals, the amount by which the cash withdrawals exceed inflows of new deposits is called: _____.

11. If an institution deals with liquidity risk by keeping extra cash or liquid assets, it is relying on: _____.

12. This is a measurement of liquidity, determined for a *portfolio* of assets. A value of 1.0 would suggest the most liquid portfolio, with values *less* than 1.0 indicating *less* liquidity.
    This measurement is called the: _____.

13. You need some cash, and you need it fast. You'll need to sell assets. To do so, you may well have to sell at a: _____.

14. A bank stands ready to liquidate transactions accounts on very short notice. The uncertainty as to exactly when depositors may withdraw cash is the essence of: _____.

15. What are two major regulator mechanisms in the U.S., aimed at insulating banks from liquidity risk?

16. Do life insurance or property-casualty insurance companies have anything analogous to FDIC insurance? Explain.

17. What is the alternative to relying on *stored liquidity*? Are there any problems or difficulties with relying on such an alternative? Explain.

Got a problem?

For **problems 1-3**, consider the balance sheets of **North Bank** and **South Bank**:

North Bank

Assets:		Liabilities:	
Cash	$ 50	Deposits	$500
Liquid securities	100		
Loans	450		
Building, fixtures	20	Equity	120
Total Assets	$620	Total Liab. & Equity	$620

South Bank

Assets:		Liabilities:	
Cash	$ 50	Deposits	$400
		Fed funds purchased	100
Loans	550		
Building, fixtures	20	Equity	120
Total Assets	$620	Total Liab. & Equity	$620

1. For both banks, compute "borrowed funds to total assets," and "loans to deposits."

2. Which bank is relying more on *stored liquidity* and which is relying more on *purchased liquidity*? Explain.

3. Suppose we want to compute a *liquidity index* for each bank—based just on financial assets (i.e., ignoring the building and fixtures). If both banks had to liquidate in *one* months' time, we will assume that: (1) they could receive 60 percent of face value on *loans*, and (2) they could receive 95 percent of face value on *securities*.

    a) Compute the liquidity index for each bank. Interpret the results.
    b) Suppose we wanted to compute such an index, based on liquidation in *three* months' time. How would you expect the resulting index number to compare with that for part (a)? (No calculating here; just explain.)

4. Suppose each bank experiences a deposit withdrawal of $40. (And, keep your answers from *problem 1* in mind.)
    a) How would the bank relying on *stored* liquidity likely respond to such a withdrawal? Show the results on the balance sheet.
    b) How would the bank relying on *purchased* liquidity likely respond to such a withdrawal? Show the results on the balance sheet.

Web cruising ideas

It can be interesting to think about the liquidity of an actual financial institution. Try the following:

1. Pick out a bank web site. (It shouldn't be too hard to find one—you'll probably have decent luck by simply typing a bank's name into your web browser.)

2. Now, look for the bank's *balance sheet*. It may be buried, amidst all the marketing hype. But look for hot buttons with terms like *annual report*, *quarterly report*, or *investor relations*. Basically, you're looking for information that is of more interest to stockholders, rather than customers. (By the way, in many cases, you will actually be at a *bank holding company* web site, and consequently, you'll find a balance sheet for *that* entity. That's okay.)

    When you find the balance sheet, look for cash, or the stuff that's "close to" cash. On the asset side: add up cash, cash items in process of collection, and deposits held in other institutions. How much are they—as a percentage of the bank's *total assets*? Also, the bank may have *federal funds sold*. You probably remember these—highly liquid, short-term loans made by the bank. Also, how big is the *investments* category—again, relative to total assets? Incidentally, you may be able to investigate the *investments* category further, especially if you are looking at the bank's annual report.   See if there is a separate schedule, detailing the security holdings. The more cash (and "cash-like") assets, relative to total assets, the more liquid is the bank.

3. One of the needs for liquidity is to pay off depositors. And, of course, the bank needs cash to do that. This motivates a classic bank ratio: the loan-to-deposits ratio. (It's pretty much self-defining, eh?) Again, you will compute it from balance sheet data. After you compute it, think about interpretation. A *lower* loan-to-deposit ratio suggests that *fewer* of the deposit dollars have been devoted to lending. And, since loans are rather illiquid, a lower ratio is an indicator of *greater* liquidity.

4. By the way, how about comparing your bank's loan-to-deposit ratio with an average figure for other banks? The FDIC summarizes a lot of that kind of summary data in its *Quarterly Banking Profile*, which is available at:

    http://www2.fdic.gov/qbp/

III. WASHING UP... AND THE "ABC" AWARDS

A. The EASIEST THING in the chapter

When it comes to measuring liquidity, *cash* is the *easiest* part. Cash is *pure liquidity*.

B. The HARDEST THING in the chapter

Frankly, it's hard for many of us in the U.S. to appreciate a *bank run*, let alone a *bank panic*. While there have been a few isolated instances in the late Twentieth Century, the dramatic events occurred well before many readers (and *this writer*) appeared on planet earth. If you're lucky enough to know folks who experienced the Great Depression, buy them a cup of coffee (some *good stuff*), and ask about their banking experiences in that era. (And also, what do they think about banks *now*?)

C. The FUNNIEST THING in the chapter... or not

Isn't the word *liquidity* funny enough?

This little word has spawned an ample supply of "word-play" over the years. You know, wonderful gems like:

> "This bank is *so darn liquid*... the CFO is wearing scuba gear."

> or...   "If this place was any *less liquid*...we'd be trading our cars for camels."

And, by the way, for you boaters in the audience... I know what you're thinking... but forget about it. It's already been done. A few years ago, one of the leading names reported for recreational watercraft was *Liquid Assets*.

IV. CHECKING THE ANSWERS... FOR SECTION II

Terms:
1. bank run
2. surrender value
3. financing gap
4. discount window
5. purchased liquidity
6. core deposits
7. BIS ladder maturity analysis
8. bank panic
9. asset side liquidity risk
10. net deposit drain
11. stored liquidity
12. liquidity index
13. fire sale price
14. liability side liquidity risk

Essays:
15. First, there is *deposit insurance*. This helps to keep "bad news" about a particular bank from triggering a bank run. If depositors are confident of the insurer's ability to make good on depositor claims, they will have no incentive to trigger a *run* on the bank. The second program is the Federal Reserve's *discount window* lending. Banks can take care of unexpected liquidity needs by borrowing from the Fed (although they do have to pledge collateral).

16. There is nothing exactly analogous to FDIC deposit insurance for the insurance industry. But there are state guarantee programs for insurance companies. These are actually administered by the private insurance companies. And, unlike FDIC insurance, there is no permanent fund established with these programs. Instead, when an insurance company has failed, the surviving insurance companies make contributions to the guarantee fund. Payments to the claimants of a failed insurance company can take considerable time.

17. A *stored liquidity* policy calls for the institution to hold more cash, or more liquid securities, which can be converted quickly to cash. An alternative policy would rely on *purchased liquidity*. With this, the institution handles liquidity needs by borrowing funds as needed. The institution's ability to borrow, of course, will depend on its standing in the credit markets. A highly risky institution will not be able to borrow in desperate times. Also, the institution relying on purchased liquidity places itself "at the mercy" of the markets, in terms of interest rates paid. Short-term rates can be especially volatile. Although the viable, healthy institution can purchase the needed liquidity, the *price paid* is a key unknown, and a source of risk.

Problems:

1. For **North Bank**:

    Borrowed funds to total assets = 0. (Because North has *no* borrowed funds.)

    Loans to deposits: $\dfrac{\$450}{\$500} = .90 = 90\%$

    For **South Bank:**

    South's "borrowed funds" are its federal funds purchased.

    Borrowed funds to total assets: $\dfrac{\$100}{\$620} = .161 = 16.1\%$

    Loans to deposits: $\dfrac{\$550}{\$400} = 1.375 = 137.5\%$

2. South Bank is relying more on *purchased liquidity*, while North Bank is relying more on *stored liquidity*. Although both banks are of the same asset size, note that South Bank has a larger loan portfolio. In contrast, North Bank holds a sizeable securities portfolio—which, in general, we would expect to be more liquid. Also, note that South Bank has fewer deposit liabilities than North Bank—and the difference is due to South Bank's federal funds purchases. South Bank's fed funds purchases are illustrative of its *purchased liquidity* policy. South Bank's loan-to-deposits ratio exceeds 100 percent, also indicative of its heavy reliance on purchased funds.

3. As indicated in the question, we are ignoring the fixed assets. So, the total *financial assets* will be $620 - $20 = $600. Also, note that *cash* is pure liquidity, so its index number is 100%, or 1.00.

    a) North's liquidity index $= \left(\dfrac{\$50}{\$600} \times 1.0\right) + \left(\dfrac{\$100}{\$600} \times .95\right) + \left(\dfrac{\$450}{\$600} \times .60\right) = .692$

    South Bank liquidity index $= \left(\dfrac{\$50}{\$600} \times 1.0\right) + \left(\dfrac{\$550}{\$600} \times .60\right) = .633$

    The liquidity index should be interpreted relative to 1.00, which represents pure liquidity. By this measurement scheme, the assets of North Bank are more liquid than those of South Bank. In a real world situation, however, keep in mind that the various loans (and securities) at the two banks might have *different* degrees of liquidity—and this would certainly affect the outcome.

b) If we deal with liquidation over a *longer* time period, we would expect to receive *bigger* portions of face value. So, the liquidity index would be *higher* (although it cannot be computed here, without more information).

4. North Bank is relying on *stored* liquidity and South Bank is relying on *purchased liquidity* (as noted in problem 1), so:

a) North Bank. *Note*: below, we're assuming that securities were liquidated. But some of the withdrawal would probably be covered from the cash account as well—in fact, as a practical matter, this is where the "hit" would first occur.

Assets:		**Liabilities:**	
Cash	$ 50	Deposits	$500
Liquid securities	100	--less withdrawal	(40)
--less sold securities	(40)		
Loans	450		
Building, fixtures	20	Equity	120
Total Assets	$580	Total Liab. & Equity	$580

b) South Bank

Assets:		**Liabilities:**	
Cash	$ 50	Deposits	$400
		--less withdrawal	(40)
		Fed funds purchased	100
Loans	550	--increased fed funds	40
Building, fixtures	20	Equity	120
Total Assets	$620	Total Liab. & Equity	$620

CHAPTER 23
MANAGING THE BALANCE SHEET III:
INTEREST RATE AND INSOLVENCY RISK

I.   SURVEYING THE TERRITORY: AN AERIAL VIEW

Note the long and impressive title here... we find ourselves *still* fiddling with the balance sheet, in a *third* installment to the story! (Heck, in the movies, it's only an occasional *Godfather* or *Harry Potter* that live beyond *one* sequel!)

Interest rates provide a pervasive source of risk. All financial institutions (maybe *all firms*?) are concerned with the cost of financing. But, financial institutions are also *holding* lots of *financial assets*. Often, these are interest rate-denominated assets—and their values will naturally be linked to interest rate movements.

There are two basic ways to look at interest rate risk. The first is a sort of "income statement" view. The question: what happens to *net income*—or components thereof—when rates change?   This is where the *repricing gap model* comes in.   The second is more of a "market value" view. The question now becomes: what happens to *values* of assets and liabilities as rates change? You might say this is a "balance sheet view"—but it's a special kind of balance sheet, one that captures *market values*. And, for this second view, we make use of the *duration* measure, introduced earlier in the text.

We also come upon insolvency risk here. Now, we are still talking about asset and liability valuation, but we don't restrict ourselves to a particular source of risk. The value changes might be prompted by interest rates changes, default risk changes... really, any of the risks we've talked about. In a sense, we are coming back to one of the basic foundations of corporation finance—concern for the value of stockholders' claims. If liability value exceeds asset value, then the firm's net worth is zero—i.e., stockholders are holding worthless claims. Perhaps this seems obvious. But it's worth discussing, because of confusion sometimes caused by the historical-sourced numbers appearing on our CPA-prepared balance sheets.

The major chapter topics:

Interest Rate and Insolvency Risk Management: Chapter Overview

Interest Rate Risk Measurement and Management

Insolvency Risk Management

II. DIGGING IN THE DIRT: A SUBTERRANEAN VIEW

Key terms

> **repricing (or funding) gap model**
> **rate sensitivity**
> **maturity buckets**
> **rate-sensitive assets**
> **rate-sensitive liabilities**
> **GAP**
> **cumulative repricing gap (CGAP)**
> **CGAP effect**
> **NII**
> **spread effect**
> **runoff**
> **duration**
> **duration gap**
> **leverage-adjusted gap**
> **convexity**
> **net worth**
> **book value**
> **market value**
> **mark-to-market**
> **book value of capital**
> **market-to-book ratio**

Got a question?

1. Loans and other assets that will be maturing, or those having interest rates which will adjust, over some specified period of time are referred to as:

   _____.

2. The difference between an institution's asset and liability values, where the values have been based on the historic or original values, is called the:

   _____.

3. The _____ is a measure showing the degree of discrepancy between valuation of a company's shares in the marketplace and the book value shown on the balance sheet.

4. Long-term loans, which might be viewed as rate *insensitive*, will produce cash flow in the short run—because of interest and principal payments. This cash flow, known as _____, is itself *rate-sensitive*.

5. When we subtract the rate sensitive liability amounts from the rate sensitive asset amounts, for *all* the various time intervals out to some specified cutoff (e.g., out to one year), we have a measurement known as:
   _____.

6. This is a short hand expression for an institution's *interest income* minus its *interest expense*.
   This is: _____.

7. This is a name given to an approach for evaluating the effects of interest rate changes on net interest income. (Note: there are actually *two* names.)
   This is the: _____.

8. In implementing the repricing gap model, we organize the various interest-denominated assets and liabilities according to the time at which they are subject to repricing. We are putting the assets and liabilities into time intervals, known as: _____.

9. The measurement known as _____ gives us the sensitivity of an asset or liability's value to small changes in interest rates.

10. Use of the duration model assumes that bond price changes are proportional to interest rate changes. In fact, however, the "price versus yield" relationship exhibits: _____.

11. In the repricing gap model, _____ is the term referring to deposits or other interest rate denominated liabilities that are subject to repricing in some specified time period.

12. If we constructed a balance sheet for an institution, but adjusted the assets and liabilities to reflect current market conditions, our balance sheet would be presented on a _____ basis.

13. Subtracting the rate sensitive liability total from the rate sensitive asset total, for a *specific* interval or maturity bucket, gives us the measure known as the:
    _____.

14. The _____ refers to the impact from a changing relationship *between* in the rate on rate-sensitive assets and the rate on rate-sensitive liabilities.

15. What is "runoff," in the context of the repricing model? Why is it a weakness, or problem, in the use of the repricing model?

16. Suppose Bank Y has a one-year cumulative repricing gap of $-24 million. Also, suppose that market interest rates should *fall* over the coming year—but there is no change in the "spread." Based on the repricing gap model, *explain* what we expect to happen to:
    a) interest income
    b) interest expense
    c) net interest income.
    (No calculations are required at this point; simply *explain*.)

17. Barnacle Bankorp has rate sensitive assets (over a one year interval) of $40 million. It has rate sensitive liabilities of $30 million. It earns an average rate of 11% on its rate-sensitive assets. It pays an average rate of 6% on its rate-sensitive liabilities. Now, suppose interest rates should *rise* over the coming year. Based on the repricing gap model, *explain*:
    a) what we expect to happen to net interest income, in the absence of any "spread effects."
    b) how spread effects could influence the outcome.

18. Northern Bank has a *leverage adjusted duration gap* of 6 years. Describe the risk it faces. Further, what could the bank do to *reduce* the risk?

19. How can an institution adjust the duration of its assets and liabilities, and hence, its duration gap?

Got a problem?

1. Consider the balance sheet of Gaping Hole Bank (in billions):

Assets		Liabilities & Equity	
Cash	$ 15	Fed funds purchased	$10
Loans: maturity < 1 year	15	Demand deposits	30
Loans: floating rate	25	CDs, maturity < 1 year	40
Loans: fixed rate, mat. > 1yr.	50	CDs, maturity > 1 year	20
Bldg. & fixtures	10	Stockholders' equity	15
Total Assets	$115	Total Liabilities & Equity	$115

    a) What is the one-year **repricing gap** for Gaping Hole?
    b) How do we interpret the answer from part (a)—what does it mean?

2. Return to essay question 16 (relating to **Bank Y**). Let's play "what if," with some *numbers*.
    a) What will happen to net interest income—on an annual basis—if rates should *fall* by 1 percent?
    b) What if rates should *rise* by 1 percent?

3. Return to essay question 17 (relating to **Barnacle Bankorp**).
   a) What will happen to Barnacle's net interest income if all rates should *increase* by 1 percentage point?
   b) What will happen to Barnacle's net interest income if the rate on assets *rises by 1 percent*, but the rate on liabilities *rises by 2 percent*?

4. Consider the simplified balance sheet below, for Durable State Bank. The entries are current market values. Also, duration numbers have already been determined, and are indicated below. The initial, average interest rate (assets and liabilities) is 8%.

Assets	Duration	**Liabilities & Equity**	Duration
Assets = $500	4	Liabilities = $460	2
		Equity = 40	
Total = $500		Total = $500	

   a) If the interest rate should *rise* by 2 percent, what will happen to the value of the Durable's assets?
   b) If the interest rate should *rise* by 2 percent, what will happen to the value of Durable's liabilities?
   c) If the interest rate should *rise* by 2 percent, what will happen to the value of Durable's equity (its net worth)?   Clue: use your answers for parts (a) and (b)
   d) If the interest rate should *fall* by 2 percent, what will happen to the value of Durable's equity?

5. Still referring to Durable State Bank (preceding problem):
   a) What is Durable's *leverage-adjusted duration gap*?
   b) Show how Durable's *duration gap* could have been used to answer problem 3, part (c).

Web cruising ideas

It can be useful to see how real banking organizations report to investors on the issue of interest rate risk. Here are two examples.

1. Banc One Corporation. They make their annual report and 10K available at the "investor relations" page of their web site:

   http://www.bankone.com/answers/BolAnswersSeg.aspx?top=all&segment=IVR

   Check out the 2001 annual report and 10K information—you can find it listed among the firm's 2002 filings with the SEC. If you look closely, you can find the company's assessment of how its earnings would be affected by a 100 basis point change in interest rates. In other words, you will see the result of a "gap-like" model calculation. Clue: I found it on page 50 of the annual report. (And yes… drinking some *strong coffee* is highly recommended before clicking around the 10K report. There are *lots* of pages and *lots* of numbers.)

2. Northern Trust Corporation. You might find the management discussion of risks especially interesting. Like Banc One, they provide the results of a "scenario analysis," indicating the expected impact of interest rate changes. I found it on page 56 of the 2001 annual report. You can get to it with the following link:

   http://www.ntrs.com/investor_relations/annual_report/index.html

III. WASHING UP... AND THE "ABC" AWARDS

A. The EASIEST THING in the chapter

The repricing gap model, even with its simplifying assumptions, is fairly straightforward. By this point, most readers are comfortable with net interest income (NII)—and that's the key variable we're watching here. What happens to NII it as interest rates on investment (e.g., loans) and funding (e.g., deposits) change? That is the question.

B. The HARDEST THING in the chapter

One difficult thing to appreciate: why do we see *both* a **repricing gap model** *and* a **duration gap model**? Is one a more general model? And, if so, wouldn't *one* model be sufficient? In a sense, the duration model is a more all encompassing model—because we look at *all* the assets and liabilities together. Also, there a clear linkage of duration gap to the value of the institution's net worth. The downside is the difficulty of measuring the duration numbers accurately. Of course, the repricing gap model has a downside as well: an inordinate degree of emphasis on a short-term variable, net interest income. But the repricing model does have a very practical thing going for it: the use of simple measures, which are easy to collect and understand.

C. The FUNNIEST THING in the chapter... or not

Some risk management terms can actually produce smiles...just think about the humor potential of words like *runoff, spread, buckets, exposure,* and *gap*.

For example...

Buckets? Who coined this high-tech term? Someone—from who knows where—decided to refer to the gap model's time intervals as *maturity buckets*. We dump our loans and deposits into the "one year bucket," the "two year bucket," and so on. Anyway, I've discovered that the mere mention of a *maturity bucket* makes people giggle. I don't know why.

How about the *"gap,"* itself? If bankers are so interested in measuring it, does that mean they *wear* it too? (I doubt it.)

Finally, what about *exposure*...? It conjures up notions of... well, suffering from sunburn, or maybe frostbite. But it's a good term, very suggestive in fact. Reduce your risk by *covering* your ... uh, let's just say *cover your vulnerable parts...* whatever and wherever they may be.

IV.   CHECKING THE ANSWERS... FOR SECTION II

Terms:
1. rate sensitive assets
2. book value of capital
3. market-to-book ratio
4. runoff
5. cumulative repricing gap (CGAP)
6. NII (or net interest income)
7. repricing gap model, or funding gap model
8. maturity buckets
9. duration
10. convexity
11. rate sensitive liabilities
12. market value, or mark-to-market value
13. GAP
14. spread effect

Essays:
15. "Runoff" occurs when a rate-*insensitive* balance sheet item actually makes periodic payments, and thus has repricing consequences. Take, for example, a long-term, fixed-rate mortgage loan. While such a loan is classified as *insensitive*, the lending institutions will be receiving payments of interest and principal. The institution will be reinvesting these receipts, and they will have to be reinvested at current market rates. Consequently, the *insensitive*, fixed-rate loan will have consequences for net interest income when interest rates are changing. So, predictions of net interest income, which ignore such runoffs, will be in error.

16. Bank Y has a *negative* gap. So, rate sensitive liabilities are *larger* than rate sensitive assets. If market rates should *fall*, then: (a) interest income will *fall*—because maturing loans and investments will be redeployed at lower interest rates, (b) interest expense will *fall*—because maturing deposits and liabilities will be refunded at lower interest rates, and (c) net interest income will *rise*—because the effects described in (b) will be of *larger magnitude* than those described in (a). In essence, the *expense savings* are more than enough to compensate for the *decreasing revenue*.

17. Barnacle's one-year gap is $40 - $30 million, or $10 million. (a) The gap is positive, so an increase in rates is expected to increase NII. (b) The "spread" is the difference between the rate earned on assets and the rate paid on liabilities. Changes in the spread can affect the outcome. If the spread increases, then the increase in NII will be even bigger than suggested in part (a). If the spread decreases, the NII could rise or fall.

18. Northern Bank has a *positive* duration gap. Its net worth is exposed to interest rate risk. The positive gap means that the duration of its assets is larger than a "weighted" duration of its liabilities. Specifically, $D_A - kD_L > 0$, where k is the ratio of the bank's liability value to its asset value. If interest rates should *rise*, then values will *fall*. And, since there is larger duration on the "asset side," the value of the bank's assets will fall by *more* than the value of its liabilities. So, its net worth will *fall*. By the same token, if interest rates should *fall*, then the bank's net worth will *rise*. To reduce the risk, Northern Bank would need to take actions that would reduce the duration gap. A duration gap of zero would mean that the bank's net worth was immunized against interest rate risk.

19. Duration is the weighted average maturity. In general, longer-maturity items will have bigger durations. (However, if a long-maturity loan is a *variable rate* loan, it is just like a short-term asset, in terms of its interest rate sensitivity.) If a bank wants to shorten the duration of its assets, it should try to make shorter-term loans, or more loans with variable rates. If it wants to lengthen its asset duration, it should make more longer-term, fixed-rate loans. It can operate similarly on the deposit side of the balance sheet. It could also influence its overall duration by its choice of securities.

Problems:

1. The textbook "guide" for is captured nicely in Table 23-2.
   a) First the rate sensitive assets (RSA): Look for anything that can be "repriced" within one year. We have:

Loans < 1 year	$15 billion
Variable rate loans	25
RSA	$40 billion

      For the rate sensitive liabilities (RSL):

Fed funds	$10 billion
CDs < 1 year	40
RSL	$50

   The "gap": RSA – RSL = $40 - $50 = $-10 (billion). The rate sensitive liabilities exceed the rate sensitive assets.

   b) With a negative gap, Gaping Hole Bank's net interest income is sensitive to market interest rate changes. In particular, the bank is poised to "win" if interest rates should *fall*. Why? If rates fall, interest revenue and interest expense will fall—but the interest expense will fall by a greater amount. (Of course, Gaping Hole is also poised to "lose" if interest rates should *rise*.)

2. Use the following:

$$\Delta NII = CGAP \times \Delta R$$

a) If rates *fall*, this becomes:

$$\Delta NII = (\$ - 24) \times (-.01) = \$.24 \text{ million}$$

This amounts to an increase of $24,000.

b) If rates *rise*, then only the sign changes, and we have a *decrease* of $.024 million.

3. For Barnacle Bankorp.
   a) Without spread effects, the story is similar to that of the preceding problem. But here, the one-year gap is positive: $40 - $30 million, or $10 million.

$$\Delta NII = (\$10) \times (.01) = \$.10 \text{ million} \quad (\text{or, an } increase \text{ of } \$10,000)$$

   b) Now, there is a "spread effect"—the spread is *decreasing*. So, use the following:

$$\Delta NII = RSA \times \Delta R_{RSA} + RSL \times \Delta R_{RSL}$$

$$\Delta NII = (\$40 \times .01) - (\$30 \times .02) = \$ - .20 \text{ million} \quad (\text{or, a } decrease \text{ of } \$20,000)$$

4. For Durable Bank:
   a) From our economic interpretation of duration, we have:

$$\Delta A = -A \times D_A \times \left(\frac{\Delta R}{1 + R} \right)$$

$$\Delta A = -\$500 \times 4 \times \left(\frac{.02}{1.08} \right) = \$ - 37.037$$

   b) On the liability side of the bank:

$$\Delta L = -L \times D_L \times \left(\frac{\Delta R}{1 + R} \right)$$

$$\Delta L = -\$460 \times 2 \times \left(\frac{.02}{1.08} \right) = \$ - 17.037$$

c) Note that *both* the asset and liability values fell. But the asset value fell by *more*. The equity (E), or net worth change is simply:

$$\Delta E = \Delta A - \Delta L = \$ - 37.037 - (\$ - 17.037) = \$ - 20.00$$

The net worth has *fallen*, as a result of the *increased* interest rate.

d) You can go back to the previous parts, and simply change a sign on the rate change. The net worth would *rise* in this scenario.

5. Still dealing with Durable Bank:
   a) The leverage adjusted duration gap:

$$D_A - kD_L = 4 - \left(460\middle/500\right) \times 2 = 2.16$$

   b) The text demonstrates that the change in net worth (E) can be expressed in terms of the duration gap:

$$\Delta E = -(D_A - kD_L) \times A \times \left(\frac{\Delta R}{1+R}\right)$$

$$\Delta E = -(2.16) \times \$500 \times \left(\frac{.02}{1.08}\right) = \$ - 20$$

We get the same answer as in problem 4, part (c).

CHAPTER 24
MANAGING RISK WITH DERIVATIVE SECURITIES

I. SURVEYING THE TERRITORY: AN AERIAL VIEW

Yes. We are still *managing risk*. But, believe it or not, we are finally getting *off* the balance sheet. You've been waiting your whole life for this, I'm sure. (Or, maybe just for the last three chapters.)

Actually, we are revisiting material from Chapter 10: *derivatives*. This includes things like call options, put options, forward contracts, and futures contracts. Now, our objective is to devote more attention to applications of these things—i.e., to the *risk management* process. Often, this means *hedging*—applying the derivatives to *reduce* our risk. The hedger has decided to take a safer path, but possibly a less lucrative one. It's sort of like the baseball player who comes to the plate, and chokes up high on the bat. The hitter is trying to increase the chance of getting wood on the ball—realizing that he *decreases* the chance of smacking one over the fence. He's willing to settle for a single.

For many financial institutions, we often think about those hedging objectives when we think of derivative use. But for the more "swashbuckling types" among us, derivatives can be used to take on risk—perhaps a calculated risk, designed to increase returns.

By the way, as something of a reminder, why do we call these things "off balance sheet" activities? Well, first think about what we see on a balance sheet. As of a particular date, you see the assets currently held, and the liabilities currently outstanding. Now, take the example of forward contract. Today, let's say some institution promises to exchange *marks* for *yen*, with delivery to occur in three months' time. The contract is established today. But the currency exchange will occur later. The institution didn't bring in any new funding *today*. And, it didn't acquire new assets *today*. So the forward contract has no impact on the balance sheet *today*.

Major chapter topics:

Derivative Securities Used to Manage risk: Chapter Overview

Forward and Futures Contracts

Options

Swaps

Comparison of Hedging Methods

Appendix A: Hedging with Futures Contracts (accessible at: **www.mhhe.com/sc2e**)

Appendix B: Hedging with Options (accessible at: **www.mhhe.com/sc2e**)

II.   DIGGING IN THE DIRT: A SUBTERRANEAN VIEW

Key terms

>   spot contract
>   forward contract
>   futures contract
>   marked to market
>   naïve hedge
>   immunized
>   microhedging
>   basis risk
>   macrohedging
>   call option
>   put option
>   short
>   long
>   CBT
>   CME
>   OTC
>   interest rate swap
>   swap buyer
>   swap seller
>   plain vanilla
>   currency swap
>   naked option
>   writing

Got a question?

1. This is a type of hedging approach which takes a "whole portfolio" view. The financial institution manager is, in essence, trying to hedge the whole balance sheet.
    This is: _____.

2. A _____ is a contract for a transaction, calling for the immediate exchange assets for funds.

3. Aside from exchange-traded option contracts, there are also _____ options.

4. An institution has written call options, and the option positions are not designed to hedge some identifiable asset or liability position.
    The institution is taking a position in: _____.

5. A _____ is an agreement for the future exchange of a specified amount of assets, at specified price. In this agreement, the buyer and seller deal directly with each other; there is no organized exchange.

6. If Jerry offers a put option contract on Microsoft stock, we can also say that Jerry is _____ put options.

7. The No-Risk National Bank has managed its on and off balance sheet positions so that it is fully hedged against interest rate movements. As a result, its profit will not be affected by interest rate movements.
   We would describe No-Risk National as being: _____.

8. When outstanding futures contracts have their prices adjusted on a daily basis, reflecting the current futures market conditions, we say that they are:
   _____.

9. This contract gives its owner the *right* to buy a specified security, at a specified price, and for a specified time. The owner, however, is *not required* to buy the specified security.
   This contract is a: _____.

10. The party who makes the floating-rate payments in an interest rate swap transaction is called the: _____.

11. When hedging with futures, _____ occurs, due to imperfect correlation of the futures price with the price of the item being hedged.

12. When an institution employs a futures or forward contract to reduce the risk exposure of a particular asset or liability, it is engaging in:
    _____.

13. If Jeff *writes* a call option, we can also say that Jeff has taken a _____ position.

14. Two parties exchange *fixed-rate payments* for *floating-rate payments*.
    This is a/an: _____.

15. Institution A agrees to send annual payments in dollars to Institution B. In exchange for this Institution B, agrees to send annual payments in Japanese yen to Institution A.
    The institutions have agreed to a: _____.

16. What *advantage* might a forward contract have, when compared with a futures contract? What *disadvantage* does the forward contract have?

17. Leigh manages a bond portfolio. She is worried about volatility in market interest rates, and is thinking about using a *futures* market transaction to protect her bond portfolio.
    a) What kind of future contract should she look for?
    b) Describe the specific kind of futures position she should take. Should it be a *long* or *short* position? What about *size*?
    c) Suppose Leigh follows your advice. Explain what happens if interest rates *rise*. What will happen if interest rates *fall*?

18. Consider Leigh's situation once again (preceding question). What if she is thinking about using an *options* market transaction for protection?
    a) What kinds of option contracts would make sense?
    b) Describe the specific kind of position she should take.
    c) Suppose Leigh follows your advice. Explain what happens if interest rates *rise*. What will happen if interest rates *fall*?

Got a problem?

1. **Jane** writes a **call option** on Ex-Corp Bond, having an exercise price of 98% of face value. The call premium is 2% of the face value of the bond. **Max** writes a **put option** on Ex-Corp Bond, also having an exercise price of 98% of face value. The put premium is 1.4% of the face value of the bond. Both options expire at the same time. Later, at the time of expiration, compute the profits of **Jane** and **Max**, if:

   a) The bond's price is 94% of face value at expiration.
   b) The bond's price is 106% of face value at expiration.

2. **Long Bank** sees some risk on its balance sheet—which it believes could be reduced with an interest rate swap. Consider the relevant part of Long Bank's balance sheet, where R_{MM} refers to the rate paid (a variable rate) on its money market deposits:

Long Bank

Assets	Liabilities
Fixed-rate loans (at 12%) $50 million	Money market deposits (at R_{MM}) $50 million

Another institution, **Short Bank**, is a possible counterparty. The relevant portion of Short Bank's balance sheet is below. Short Bank's loan rate is tied to LIBOR.

Short Bank

Assets	Liabilities
Floating-rate loans (at LIBOR) $50 million	Fixed-rate deposits (at 6%) $50 million

a) What specific kind of swap arrangement should Long Bank try to get with Short Bank?

b) Assuming the banks agree to the swap, show (annualized) interest income and interest expense for each bank. Has Long Bank reduced its risk?

c) Is there any remaining risk for Long Bank or Short Bank?

3. Consider the simplified balance sheet below, for **Great Lake Bancorp**. Duration measurements have also been shown, in parentheses.

Assets:		Liabilities & Net Worth:		
Loans & investments (8)	$250million	Deposits	(2)	$230
		Net worth		20
Total	$250	Total		$250

a) Compute the bank's *duration gap*.

b) Interpret this duration gap—what does it suggest about the bank's exposure to interest rate risk.

c) If the bank were attempting to use futures for *macrohedging*, what explain what sort of position would be required.

d) If the bank wanted to hedge by using swaps, explain what sort of position would be required.

Web cruising ideas

1. The Chicago Mercantile Exchange has part of its web site devoted to hedging with its interest rate futures products. Naturally, they would love to sell you on their particular brand of stuff… but even so, this can be a useful educational device. You can find it at:

   http://www.cme.com/

2. You can also find some basics about using calls and puts at the Chicago Board Options Exchange's site:

   http://www.cboe.com/Home/Default.asp

III.   WASHING UP... AND THE "ABC" AWARDS

A. The EASIEST THING in the chapter

The easy thing is that we're working with some familiar animals here. We've been to this zoo before. Now, we're just trying to learn how to do some tricks with them—without getting bitten.

B. The HARDEST THING in the chapter

You will notice that there are various ways of accomplishing the same purpose. If you need protection from interest rate movements, for example—you can use futures, swaps, and options. What governs your choice? This can be hard to understand at a *textbook* level. To some extent, these alternative markets may be redundant. But, there is a good chance that the various activities emerged in the marketplace because they offered some unique advantages—at least for some market participants.

C. The FUNNIEST THING in the chapter... or not

"Gee, Professor Ivory-Tower, I only left off the minus sign in my answer. Everything else was right. But you deducted fifteen points from my score!"

Ever been in this situation—and felt that same sense of moral outrage? Well, listen to my story...

I can't quote "chapter and verse" on this. It was handed down to me by someone who served on the board of directors for a depository institution. The institution had started to use futures contracts as a hedging device. A risk manager—although he probably did not have such a fancy title back then—carefully worked out the required number of contracts for the desired hedging objective. Unfortunately, when all was said and done, the institution had experienced a "double-whammy." It had *lost* money—*both* from its "on the balance sheet" matters, *and* from the futures position. What happened? Although the manager had computed the *size* of his position correctly, *he got the sign wrong*. He had entered the futures market on the *wrong side*. In essence, he had doubled up on risk!

Sometimes, in practice, that silly little sign *really matters*.

(By the way... just think...if the market had gone "the other way," our mathematically challenged risk manager would have looked like a *genius*.)

IV.   CHECKING THE ANSWERS... FOR SECTION II

Terms:

1. macrohedging
2. spot contract
3. OTC (for over-the-counter)
4. naked options
5. forward contract
6. writing
7. immunized
8. marked to market
9. call option
10. swap seller
11. basis risk
12. microhedging
13. short
14. interest rate swap
15. currency swap

Essays:

16. A *forward contract* is a bilateral agreement—two parties negotiate the deal. As such, the two parties can negotiate for specific provisions, "tailor-made" to handle their specific needs. For example, a hedger might desire to deliver a specific kind of asset, in a specific quantity, and at a specific date in the future. And, the specifics desired by the hedger might not be well served by available *futures contracts*, with their particular standardized features. However, the advantage of a tailor-made contract also brings with it a significant disadvantage. The *liquidity* of such a contract will be very limited. So, if one party would want to "get out" of the contract early, it may be difficult to find another party willing to strike a deal, taking over the position. It's very much analogous to the problem of having a custom-built house, but one designed in a peculiar, non-standard way (maybe a purple polka dot motif throughout). The house may serve the needs of the original inhabitants very nicely—those purple polka dot lovers—but if it's viewed as an "oddball" house, its marketability will be limited.

17. Leigh's bonds will fall in value if interest rates should *rise*.

    a) Leigh should look for a futures contract written on something similar to her bond portfolio. Obviously, this suggests contracts written on bonds. She will also want to consider the features of her bond portfolio. If her bonds are long-term, for example, she will want a contract written on long-term bonds—like a Treasury bond contract.

    b) Leigh will want to *sell* the futures contracts. A hedger will want to take a position *opposite* to the position she is trying to hedge. Leigh has *purchased* bonds, so she needs to *sell* the futures. How much? It depends. If she is *naively* hedging, she will sell enough contracts to match the size of her bond holdings. However, she might decide to hedge only partially—using a lesser number of contracts. Also, if she digs into the details of how the contract's price will move in relation to her bond portfolio value, she can adjust her futures position accordingly.

c) If market rates *rise*, the value of Leigh's bonds will *fall*. But, she has locked in a price for delivery of bonds, through her futures position. Since market bond prices have fallen, Leigh's contract to deliver—at a predetermined price—becomes valuable. She gains on the futures contract, thereby offsetting the losses on her bond portfolio. If, on the other hand, interest rates *fall*, Leigh's bonds will rise in value. But, of course, she has a *short* futures position—and that position will *lose*. Note: even though Leigh might have "regrets" if she encounters this latter scenario, it's still a *hedged* situation.

18. Leigh has the same problem—we are merely thinking about the use of a different kind of derivative.

a) Leigh would want to use options written on bonds. (Or, she might well use options written on bond *futures*.) The main point is that she would want an option contract that is likely to "behave" in a predictable way *relative to* her bond portfolio.

b) One way would be to *buy* a *put* on a bond (or possibly put on a bond *future*). A second way would be to *sell ("write") a call* on a bond.

c) *If she bought a put*: If interest rates rise, causing Leigh's portfolio to lose value, then the bonds underlying the put contract will be losing value too. This, in turn, will make Leigh's put option more valuable, and it will offset the loss on her bond portfolio. If interest rates fall, then bond values are rising. Leigh will not exercise her put option. She reaps gains on her bond portfolio, although the gains are diminished by the premium she had to pay for the put.

If she wrote a call: If interest rates rise, the lower bond values mean that the call will not be exercised. Leigh has received a premium for selling the call, however, which helps to offset the losses on her bond portfolio. Note, however, that the premium is a fixed amount—it does not rise if losses on her bond portfolio mount. If interest rates fall, then the call is likely to be exercised—and this will mean losses to Leigh, as she "makes good" on her written call contract. The losses will offset the gains she is experiencing on her bond portfolio.

Problems:

1. Compute profits as a percentage of the bond's face value.
   a) If the bond price ends up at **94%** of face:

   Jane received 2% of face value when writing her call. Since the bond price is lower than the exercise price, the call will *not* be exercised. Jane's profit will simply be the **2%** premium (applied to face value).

   Max's put option *will* be exercised. Max will have to buy the bond for a price of 98% (of face), even though it is only worth 94% right now. Of course, he keeps the 1.4% premium he received initially. Max's profit (or loss) will be: 1.4% - (98% - 94%) = **-2.6%** (of face value).

   b) If the bond price is **106%** of face:

   Jane's written call *will* be exercised. Jane keeps her 2% premium, but she must sell the bond for 98%, well below its current value. Jane's profit (or loss) will be: 2% - (106% - 98%) = **-6%** (of face value)

   Max's written put will *not* be exercised. Max keeps his **1.4%** premium, which is his profit (again, as a percent of face value).

2. Long Bank/Short Bank:
   a) The bank is confronted with interest rate risk. Its variable rate deposits could become more costly, but its interest income from loans is fixed. To reduce the risk, it needs to arrange a swap whereby it *pays fixed-rate amounts*, while *receiving floating-rate amounts*—by convention, such a party would be called the "swap buyer." Of course, Long Bank needs to find a counter-party willing to take the opposite side of such a transaction—a "swap seller." It just so happens that Short Bank is a likely candidate—since it faces the "reverse problem."

   b) We are assuming that Long Bank negotiates a deal for a *notional* amount of $50 million.

   Long Bank:
   On balance sheet

Income on loans	+12% X $50 million
Expense of money mkt. deposits	$-R_{MM}$ X $50 million
From the swap	
Payment (fixed rate)	-12% X $50 million
Receipt (floating rate)	+LIBOR X $50 million
Total	$50 million X $(LIBOR - R_{MM})$

<u>Short Bank:</u>
On balance sheet

Income on loans	LIBOR X $50 million
Expense of deposits	-6% X $50 million

From the swap

Payment (floating rate)	-LIBOR X $50 million
<u>Receipt (fixed rate)</u>	<u>+12% X $50 million</u>
Total	$50 million X (12% – 6%) = $3 million

Both banks have reduced interest rate risk. Short Bank has "locked in" a spread of 6%, which translates to $3 million on an annual basis. Long Bank has locked in something that may seem a bit less certain—the difference between LIBOR and the rate on money market deposits. But that is still less risky than what it started with—because the two rates are likely to be positively correlated.

c) There is the possibility that a bank will not live up to the agreement—in other words, there is credit, or default risk. Also, in view of the comment just made in part (b), Long Bank faces some uncertainty as to how closely LIBOR and R_{MM} will move together. This is really just like the "basis risk" discussed in the context of futures contracts.

3. For Great Lake Bank:

a) The duration gap: $= D_A - kD_L$ (where k = liabilities/assets)

$$= 8 - \left(\frac{230}{250} \times 2 \right) = 6.16$$

b) The duration gap is *positive*, indicating that the assets of the bank have higher duration than the (weighted) liabilities. There is more sensitivity, in other words, on the *asset* side of the balance sheet. The bank is poised to "win" if interest rates *fall*, but to "lose" if interest rates should *rise*.

c) The bank could offset some of its "asset sensitivity" by *selling* futures contracts—contracts written on bonds. If interest rate should rise, the futures contracts would pay off, helping to offset the effects of the positive duration gap.

d) To handle the risk with a swap agreement, the bank would want to *pay fixed rate* and *receive floating rate*—i.e., it would be on the "buy side" of a swap agreement.

CHAPTER 25
LOAN SALES AND ASSET SECURITIZATION

I.   SURVEYING THE TERRITORY: AN AERIAL VIEW

Believe it or not, we find ourselves at the final frontier. After mastering Chapter 25, you will be a certified, homogenized… *smart* person. (Well… you'll at least be smart about matters of financial markets and institutions.)

The topic in Chapter 25 is basically how lending institutions can *remove* loans from the balance sheet. Of course, the loans don't disappear, into thin air. Instead, they end up on the balance sheets of *others*. In the process, a given loan may get split up into pieces (as with a *loan sale*), or pooled with other loans (as with a *securitized* loan).

There's a certain irony to all this. Back in Chapter 21, we were thinking about collecting and analyzing data…doing the analysis that finally results in loans being made. The idea was to try to do a better job of making loans than the bank across town. But now that we've *made* the loans… well, in Chapter 25 we start talking about *unloading* them. *"Yes, this is a good loan request. Let's do the deal. Okay… now let's get rid of it… and get it off our balance sheet."*

Why? The answer has a lot to do with efficiency. Who can best *originate* the loans? Who is best suited to *invest* in the loans? And who is best at *servicing* the loans? The answers to these questions may not be the same party. That's the essence of loan sales and securitization activities: dividing things or combining things into efficient units…or maybe efficient tasks.

Much of Chapter 25 will be reminiscent of things covered before. *Securitization* is the construction of a particular *derivative* security (the topic of Chapter 10). And the most popular loans for securitization have been *mortgage* loans (the topic of Chapter 7). Further, what do you end up with, *after* the securitization? Well, it walks and talks very much like a *bond* (the topic of Chapter 6). It's all starting to feel like a walk down memory lane, eh? Chapter 25 is clearly linked to lots of things we've already covered—and that seems very appropriate for the last chapter of the book.

Why Financial Institutions Securitize Assets: Chapter Overview

Loan Sales

Loan Securitization

Securitization of Other Assets

Can All Assets Be Securitized?

II. DIGGING IN THE DIRT: A SUBTERRANEAN VIEW

Key terms

asset securitization
corresponding banking
highly leveraged transaction (HLT) loan
bank loan sale
recourse
participation in a loan
assignment
LDC loans
financial distress
vulture fund
downsizing
Brady bond
fraudulent conveyance
Ginnie Mae (GNMA)
Fannie Mae (FNMA)
Freddie Mac (FHLMC)
fully amortized
prepay
pass through
collateralized mortgage obligation (CMO)
REMIC
mortgage-backed bond (MBB)
asset-backed bonds
CARDs

Got a question?

1. Home mortgage borrowers can payoff their loans early, or _____ the mortgages, and this is especially likely if current mortgage rates are below mortgage coupon rates.

2. _____ is a government-owned agency, with two major functions: sponsoring mortgage-backed securities programs and guaranteeing the timely pass-through of principal and interest payments to investors.

3. A _____ is used to finance leveraged buyouts and mergers and acquisitions.

4. If a financial institution sells a loan to another institution *without* _____, then the selling institution removes the loan from its balances sheet. It has no liability if the loan should eventually go bad.

5. When the economic situation of a borrower is such that timely payments (on bonds or loans outstanding) cannot be made, we describe the borrower as being in: _____.

6. The relationship between banks, whereby a relatively large bank provides various services to a smaller bank, is called: _____.

7. Loans to certain Asian, African, and Latin American countries have been referred to as: _____.

8. When residential mortgage securitized by the issuance of GNMA _____ securities, all the monthly payments made by the mortgage borrowers will flow back to the purchasers of the GNMA securities.

9. This type of securitization vehicle has multiple classes of claims; the different classes have their payments determined in different ways.
This is the: _____.

10. This provides an example of securitization, but applied to non-mortgage assets—in particular, credit carding lending.
These are called: _____.

11. This describes a type of loan sale in which the buyer is not a party to the underlying credit agreement. Also, the buyer exercises only partial control over changes in loan contract's terms.
This is a: _____.

12. The so-called _____ are specialized investment funds established to invest in distressed loans.

13. The _____ is a bond developed under a U.S. Treasury plan, which allows less developed countries to convert (or "swap") their loans into more liquid bonds.

14. A/an _____ refers to the purchase of a share of a loan. One key feature is the transfer of all rights upon the sale, so that the loan buyer holds a direct claim on the borrower.

15. What is the advantage, to *investors*, of the CMO method of securitization?

16. What is the advantage of the CMO method to the party who structures and issues the CMO claims?

17. What are the key issues in determining whether securitization will become successful for non-mortgage lending?

18. Why would a loan participation present a "double risk" situation to the buyer?

19. The text refers to counterparty and "moral hazard" risk, in the context of loan sales. Explain this.

Got a problem?

1. Bank-25 has made a $7 million to a commercial customer. There are 6 years left until maturity, and the principal is due entirely at maturity. Annual interest payments, at 9%, are required at the end of each year. The borrower's position has deteriorated since the loan was made; a market interest rate of 13% would be appropriate if the loan were being negotiated right now. If Bank-25 were to sell this loan, what value might it expect?

2. Last Bank has a $5 million loan outstanding. The loan has 4 years left until maturity, and the borrower makes end-of-year interest payments at 10% of the loan balance. The principal is due entirely at maturity. Last Bank is thinking about selling the loan.
   a) If it sells *with recourse*, Last Bank can sell the loan at a price consistent with a 10.7% yield. What price would Last Bank receive?
   b) If it sells *without recourse*, Last Bank can sell the loan at a price consistent with an 11% yield. What price would Last Bank receive?

3. Consider a bank with the following balance sheet:

Assets:		Liabilities:	
Cash	$ 200	Deposits	$3,300
U.S. Treas. Sec.	500		
Loans	2,800	Capital	200
Total Assets	$ 3,500	Total Liab. & Cap.	$3,500

The bank faces the following regulated capital requirement: it must maintain capital equal to 8% of its loans. Its cash and U.S. Treasury holdings require *no* regulatory capital.

Is the bank in compliance with the capital requirement? If it is, how much "extra capital" does it have? If it is *not*, indicate what the bank could do to bring itself into compliance—and show how the balance sheet might change.

4. A savings institution has the balance sheet below.

Assets:		Liabilities:	
Cash	$ 70	Deposits	$300
Mortgage loans	280	Capital	50
Total Assets	$ 350	Total Liab. & Cap.	$350

Suppose the institution decides to issue mortgage-backed bonds. It finds it can issue $200 in bonds, by putting up $230 of its mortgages as collateral.

a) Show the balance sheet of the institution, immediately after the bonds are issued.]
b) What might happen at this point, prompting further change on the balance sheet?
c) Why would the institution want to issue the bonds?

Web cruising ideas

1. Ginnie Mae has an informative web site. You might especially be interested in its information for *investors*.

   http://www.ginniemae.gov

2. You can also find some good descriptive information on mortgage-backed securities at HUD's site (Department of Housing and Urban Development). And you will see some discussion of the "REMIC" (for Real Estate Mortgage Investment Conduit). Find it at:

   http://www.hud.gov/progdesc/mbs-ms.htl

III. WASHING UP... AND THE "ABC" AWARDS

A. The EASIEST THING in the chapter

We find ourselves dealing with *loans* again. And, we're dealing with *bonds* again, too. We're sort of blending together things that have been covered before. The language should be familiar by now. *(We've got no excuses.)*

B. The HARDEST THING in the chapter

The hardest thing would be the "nuts and bolts" of the CMO vehicle: both the rationale for the multiple tranches—and how the payments get divided up among various claimants. (And, oh yeah...maybe also...why do you suppose they referred to the classes as *tranche*s, in the first place? Maybe someone was trying to impress us by adding a little international flavor to the lingo, perhaps?)

C. The FUNNIEST THING in the chapter... or not

Well, those wild and crazy folks at Ginnie Mae seem to have a sense of humor. Or at least they're trying...

At the Ginnie Mae web site (noted earlier), there is a section for *kids*. It's populated with cartoon characters—having names like *Remmick* and *Ginnie*, of course. You'll find games there... and what are described as *cool stories*. I confess: I did not read the *cool stories*. (And somehow, I doubt they have a whole lot to do with stuff like CMOs—but who knows?)

There might be a downside to all this, however. Introduce a site like this to the little ones in your vicinity... and you may be peppered with a couple hundred questions... about mortgage-backed bonds, REMICs, and the like. But that's not the worst of it. Kids catch on fast. Just wait till they start *correcting* you, based on their newly acquired wisdom. Maybe we should just leave them to their *non*-mortgage-backed games.

IV. CHECKING THE ANSWERS... FOR SECTION II

Terms:

1. prepay
2. Ginnie Mae (GNMA, or Government National Mortgage Association)
3. highly leveraged transaction (HLT) loan
4. recourse
5. financial distress
6. correspondent banking
7. LDC loans
8. pass throughs
9. collateralized mortgage obligations (CMOs)
10. CARDs
11. participation in a loan
12. vulture funds
13. Brady bond
14. assignment

Essays:

15. A CMO is a multiclass sort of pass-through security. Buyers of the securities in different classes have different promised coupon rates. Prepayments are allocated so that, at any one time, just one class of the CMO will experience early retirement of their claims. Other classes are protected from the prepayment risk, at least for a time. The CMO structure serves to distribute the risk. Investors have greater certainty as to the prepayment risk they face, in a given class.

16. The CMO amounts to a "repackaging" of existing claims. For example, an issue of Ginnie Mae pass-throughs is bought up, and several classes of claims are issued against it. The party who engineers the repackaging is hoping to "add value," by selling CMO claims for something more than the Ginnie Mae pass-throughs. This is possible if the repackaged claims better serve the demands of investors.

17. It is more costly to securitize loans that are not homogeneous in their characteristics. For example, mortgage loans have become fairly standardized—in terms of maturity, the type of collateral, payment structure, etc. Also, there is secondary market activity for the collateral. As a result, mortgages lend themselves nicely to the "packaging" that goes on with securitization. On the other hand, commercial loans can have many different maturities, unique loan covenants, and widely differing collateral types. The prospects for widespread securitization of such loans are less certain.

18. The "buying" institution in a participation is obviously concerned with the credit quality of the underlying loan. But, in addition, the buying institution must have some concern for the safety of the originating lender—the institution who is offering the loan, through participation. If this "selling" bank should fail, then the

"buying" institution may be in the position of an unsecured creditor. In such a scenario, the "buying" bank would not have sole claim to its share of the original, underlying loan.

19. When loans are offered for sale, the buyer needs to be wary about the *quality* what is being offered. The seller may try to "unload" the higher risk loans, without explicitly identifying them as such.

Problems:

1. The cash flow pattern here is a simple one—just like that for a coupon-paying bond, where the "coupon" is $7 million times 9%, or $0.63 million. Discount the six interest payments and the year-6 principal amount, at 13%:

$$PV = \frac{\$0.63m}{(1.13)} + \frac{\$0.63m}{(1.13)^2} + ... + \frac{\$0.63m + \$7M}{(1.13)^6} = \$5.881m$$

2. Here, the annual interest payment is 10% of $5 million, or $0.5 million. Discount these interest payments, as well as the year-4 principal payment, at the two alternative interest rates.

a) With recourse:

$$PV = \frac{\$0.5m}{(1.107)} + \frac{\$0.5m}{(1.107)^2} + \frac{\$0.5m}{(1.107)^3} + \frac{\$0.5m + \$5m}{(1.107)^4} = \$4.892m$$

b) Without recourse:

$$PV = \frac{\$0.5m}{(1.11)} + \frac{\$0.5m}{(1.11)^2} + \frac{\$0.5m}{(1.11)^3} + \frac{\$0.5m + \$5m}{(1.11)^4} = \$4.845Mm$$

Of course, it makes sense that buyers would be willing to pay *more* if there is recourse.

3. The required capital is 8% of the loan amount of $2,800, or $224. The bank is deficient in its capital, since it has only $200. To bring itself into compliance, it could: (1) sell $24 more in stock, thereby increasing its capital—with the proceeds to be placed in cash or U.S. Treasury securities (or other things that don't require capital), or (2) sell some loans—in particular, it would need to sell $300 in loans, to make its existing capital ($200) exactly equal to 8% of its loan value. This second alternative is shown below—with the $300 from the loan sale being invested in Treasury securities.

Assets:		Liabilities:	
Cash	$ 200	Deposits	$3,300
U.S. Treas. Sec.	800		
Loans	2,500	Capital	200
Total Assets	$ 3,500	Total Liab. & Cap.	$3,500

4. All of the mortgages remain on the institution's balance sheet, but now some of them are segregated, serving as collateral for the newly issued bonds.

a) First, below is the balance sheet, immediately after the bond issuance:

Assets:		Liabilities:	
Cash	$ 270	Deposits	$300
Mortgages (collateral)	230	Mortgage-backed bonds	200
Mortgages	50	Capital	50
Total Assets	$550	Total Liab. & Cap.	$550

b) The cash proceeds could then be used for: (1) investing—either in securities or new loans, or (2) to pay off some depositors. Probably some combination of both would occur.

c) Before the issuance of the bonds, the institution was probably subject to significant interest rate risk. Deposits generally have much shorter maturities than mortgages. The issuance of the bonds can help the institution to reduce this risk, by achieve a better "match" of maturities between the left and right side of the balance sheet.

NOTES

NOTES

NOTES

NOTES

NOTES

NOTES

NOTES